To Hugh Cairns,

Taking joy in life with
good food and drinks!
Cheers   Whisky Buff Bob

Single Malt Flavours

To my friend Hugh
the 7th of november 2011.

Dan

Bob Minnekeer

Single Malt Flavours

COOKING WITH HERBS AND SPICES ON WHISKY

Recipes: Stef Roesbeke & Bob Minnekeer
Photographs: Andrew Verschetze & Joris Devos

LANNOO

THE TRIPLE DISTILLED

AUCHENTOSHAN

SINGLE MALT SCOTCH WHISK

A finest Lowland Malt, produced in
SCOTLAND since 1823, under the watchful
eye of the Distillery Manager

12

The **TRIPLE DISTILLED** award winning,
extra smooth, SINGLE MALT renowned
for its soft, delicate flavour

40%alc/vol.

MATURED FOR OVER TWELVE YEARS
DISTILLED AND BOTTLED IN SCOTLAND

700ml e

THE TRIPLE DIS

AUCHENT

SINGLE MALT

40%alc/vol.

Contents

> An endless search for healthy flavourings

Changing times continually demand new approaches to all kinds of things. This applies just as much to whisky and to experiencing the pleasure of sniffing and tasting. Going along with the current hype, supported by the availability of products worldwide, for which the last half century has opened up an incredible treasury of miscellaneous items, is not only a possibility but in fact essential. The cross-fertilization between all continents and cultures has greatly encouraged this.

In this book we approach the subject of whisky from an entirely new angle, but in doing so we again offer full information for both experts and neophytes.

It is a fact that in our regions cooking and eating tasty but healthy food has become one of the most important hobbies, or even the most important hobby.
This growing and flourishing industry has certainly heavily influenced the behaviour of people in the last fifty years. Obviously greater prosperity also brings an increase of consumption with it for the ordinary citizen.
The number of restaurants rose steadily during this period to meet this demand for consumption. Employment in this sector today is substantial, and can be regarded as essential. Hotel schools and all kinds of culinary courses stimulate the author's Burgundian nation still more.

All television channels bring cooking at all levels into the living room. Sometimes in intolerable versions that make the real gourmet's hair stand on end. It is a hype, certainly, but there is no reason why it shouldn't be both innovative and well-thought-out, and yes, as healthy as possible. Our top chefs know very well what they are doing and produce very good, educational and even relaxing programmes, which will certainly interest the hobby cook.

Because we consider gastronomy so important and have the opportunity to visit countless restaurants and bistros, there will always be a potential temptation to overdo things. This would certainly be at the cost of our health.
This means that we have to be enormously circumspect in the way in which we deal with a variety of foodstuffs that expose our constitution to all sorts of dangers as a result of an excess of them.
To safeguard our health as much as possible, it is high time to be very well informed about all the opportunities we are offered.

Highly trained chefs don't let a single opportunity pass of bringing healthy and well-balanced food to the table (even at elaborate dinners). At the same time they use their unlimited creativity more than ever to stimulate our senses to the utmost and to let us enjoy it even more intensely.

> The reason for this work

A few years ago a good acquaintance remarked that for him, on the advice of his doctor, the use of fats and oils was practically over.
Olive oil to improve the taste of a salad, all kinds of cream sauces, herb or garlic butter, and so on, were no longer for him.
This gave me the idea of developing applications with herbal extracts on a single malt. To replace oils by whisky did not seem to be an insurmountable obstacle.

Personally I also had a problem to deal with. I could simply not digest a single dish in which paprikas were used, whether fried, steamed or prepared in any other way. And this when I actually like the taste of paprikas very much.

As a connoisseur of single malt whisky I very soon developed the idea to extract aromas of herbs and spices by and with a matching malt whisky. The urge to work out this concept for various applications imposed itself automatically. Not only to replace the existing herb oils, but certainly also to give dishes an added value by means of the extra aromas which we could create with these applications
I knew that this would not be a simple matter, but the result is really astonishing. Apart from being able to use the flavours of products that were not easy to digest, this new method offers no end of possibilities and applications to aromatize all kinds of dishes with these extracts. And this without the use of fattening sauces.

This work is in fact a do-it-yourself book, supplemented with examples and applications, which will enable everyone to compose their own assortment of single malt herbal extracts.
The years of research and tests have given me so much satisfaction that I definitely wanted to share it with others. In this book, working together with chef Stef Roesbeke, we process an assortment of herbs and spices regularly used in our everyday kitchen. For each extract we make, carefully worked out applications are mentioned. For the selected extracts herbs and spices commonly in use have been chosen, but obviously this collection is never complete.

As soon as you are familiar with this technique, and can make use of the experience you have acquired while using this 'do-it-yourself' book, you can make your own aromas of your personal choice from the selection of spices, flavourings and herbs.

Your own creativity, adapted to your own preference, offers an ocean of possibilities. Southern, Eastern, mild, spicy... all kinds of combinations, you name it, the possibilities are simply endless.

Whisky has in fact, just like herbs and spices, conquered the world. The popularity of herbs, spices and this drink has no equal. This is clearly due to the diversity in flavours.

> Herbs and spices with their added value

The current supply of products, whether or not based on a healthy production, is immeasurably great. All respectable food outlets, supermarkets, drugstores or pharmacies offer a wide assortment of such products.

It is impossible to open a newspaper or magazine without being inundated with advertisements about all kinds of complaints and the appropriate curative tea or pills based on herbs.

Of course there will be some very good products, and made in good faith, on the market. But at the same time the fear is not unfounded that profitability makes it very difficult to assess this market. Stimulating love potions based on herbs are praised sky high, but rarely produce the promised result. Advice from people with expert knowledge is always very welcome. Practising medicine in this area will certainly lead the consumer in the right direction.

Diversity of tastes in food

For us the most important aspect is that the aroma and the taste of herbs and spices give extra dimensions to the dishes, making them richer in taste, and more balanced and/or more pronounced. In other words, that they are asking to be consumed.

Moreover, in this work we concentrate mainly on applications in our everyday cuisine.

In the knowledge that a balanced diet is the basis of everything, we have worked some health tips into our recipes and applications.

Misplaced use

During battles and wars, when food was scarce or arrived late at the front, herbs have been used to disguise the taste of bad meat.

An overwhelming supply

A sector still growing is the cultivation and sales of herbs and spices, both fresh and dried. Globally the commercial value of these products has led to several wars and colonizations. Fortunately it is now possible to have access to the world supply virtually everywhere.

Very many books have already come on the market which discuss the subject of 'herbs and spices' in great detail. In this book we approach this subject from an entirely new angle.

Since the origin of the human race the medicinal qualities of extracts of herbs and spices have been known. In all cultures and civilizations there were, and still are, healers and magicians who have used this knowledge.

> Your own whisky bar and your own herb garden

Set up your own whisky bar with a sufficient diversity of flavours. In addition, lay out your own herb garden.

This last is by no means an impossible task.
It can simply be done in a corner of the vegetable garden, but just as well on a balcony or in a plant pot on a terrace or in a shelter. It is even possible inside the house.
It is important that the herbs are protected from the wind, are in a sunny position and don't get too much water.

While processing or preparing them it is advisable not to pick too much from a plant. It is better to take small quantities as you need them.

If the plant grows too large, then in most cases drying or preserving the herbs is the best solution. Certainly dried herbs need not be considered inferior to fresh ones. Here it is mainly a matter of different preparations and applications.

A private herb garden also offers the opportunity of always being able to pick fresh herbs and sometimes make use of the aromas on offer without needing to do anything to them. For instance, just to create the right atmosphere in the room with their scents.

> Why herbs on single malt whisky?

One of the disadvantages of fresh herbs, spices and other flavourings is the short time they will keep. Generally herbs have to be very freshly cut to give the best result during the preparation of dishes.

The extraction of all these flavours by using whisky can, of course, be done as soon as the plant is ready for it. The result is that there is little or no loss.
The storage time varies and can in the right circumstances be quite long. Exposing them to sunlight obviously affects the colour, and the flavours can weaken a little after some time. This is why it is advisable always to make a quantity that can be used up within a few months.

It is obvious that not all flavourings, spices and herbs are suitable for all applications. This also applies to the production of extracts on whisky.

We often find herbs which have been soaked in various oils in many different applications and easily available. In this way it is just as possible to get perfect proportions of taste and balance, but the basic ingredient still obviously remains oil.

Not all herbs release their tastes and aromas entirely when using this procedure. That means that certain herbs or spices have to be approached differently to reach the desired result.

To find this harmony is certainly no easier or simpler when extracting flavours and aromas from herbs or spices with whisky. But you do get a result faster than with oil. There is the additional advantage that the flavours and aromas that are released are more pronounced.
The combination of two perfect products full of flavour of the right choice and in the right proportions results in an unbelievable explosion of taste and aroma.
To season dishes with herbs without using whisky or oi aims at a different result and application.

The advantages of this process

The use of vaporizers allows a nice even spread over the dishes and makes it easy to apply a perfect dosage. In this way you can, for instance, give scampi an aniseed-whisky aroma. The speed with which the chef can spray the dishes in the kitchen, or even at the table, is an extra trump card.

To add a perfume to a fattening sauce is one of the many advantages of these whisky-and-herbs scents. Just think of the variety of cream sauces which can be partly replaced by it, or of the diversity you can create with it.

After a dish has been prepared, each guest has the opportunity to add an aroma to a dish to his own taste. Everyone at the table can determine his own preference without his fellow guests having to taste the same flavour. This would, for example, allow everyone at the table to season part of a roast to his own choice. Garlic, pepper, marjoram, tarragon, whatever they want. With fresh herbs, without extracting them, you could not possibly reach the same results.

The scent of garlic will not settle on your breath as much if a garlic scent has been used after the food has been prepared.

Fresh herbs and/or vegetables (for instance paprika) which lead to digestive problems for some people, don't cause these problems if they are offered in the shape of a whisky scent.

By allowing an aroma to flow across a dish by means of a pipette, you can still create the sensation of a sauce.

Because of the alcohol you get more of a taste, and a more intense taste, with fewer herbs.

Less sauce clearly means fewer calories.

> More intensive enjoyment

But above all it is the enrichment of experiencing the aromas which is very important. Just think how the atmosphere around you can be influenced by scented candles or the effect on your brain of eucalyptus scent in the vapour of a Turkish bath.

Insects are attracted not only by the bright colours of flowers, but just as much by the strong scents these plants and flowers spread around.

People take all these beautiful experiences too much for granted; we notice them, but we could enjoy them much more intensely. We walk through a wood and experience these pleasant wood scents as calming and stress-reducing. The scent of flowers in a florist's shop can take some people into a totally different atmosphere. The smell of chlorine in a swimming pool makes everything seem much cleaner, and if somewhere something is being cleaned with bleach, it instils a familiar sense of hygiene.

In the same way herb and spice aromas will very soon and strongly stimulate the nose and the senses through the quick alcoholic vaporization.

You may assume from this that scent occupies centre stage and that we are extending the experience around it. Just as you might, for instance, walk through a beautiful flower garden and take in all the pleasant scents and the attractive-looking shrubs, while listening to the melodious whistling of a song bird.

This can create the perfect atmosphere to let all your senses enjoy it fully and at the same time. And that can allow you to enjoy more without overdoing it.

The right combination of a dish that looks beautiful, is perfectly seasoned and in addition has complementary aromas in its immediate surroundings, allows all three senses to enjoy at the same moment. At the same time the touch of a velvet-soft tablecloth, table napkin, decoration, crystal glasses, and cutlery, accompanied by the right musical background, offer a simultaneous enjoyment. Playing on the five senses and letting them enjoy at one and the same moment is the object here.

> Influencing the senses or the theatre of the senses

We happen to live in a society where suggestion and illusion set the tone. This influences the pattern of our lives every day.

Our senses absorb all kinds of advertising spots and visual presentations of top products. I don't think anyone can say that he has never been taken in or that the wine he had on holiday wasn't really so very nice.

With all these illusionary suggestions people will inevitably sometimes take the wrong decisions.

And the following experiment proves that the senses are very easily influenced.

Ask someone to taste a white or red wine in a light tunnel. Talk convincingly to the taster every time the light changes colour.

The right remarks will automatically call up illusions for the taster, making him or her experience better or less good tastes.

In clear, neutral light the description of the drink under discussion is introduced, and everything will be experienced by them as it has been described.

When the light changes to azure blue the drink suddenly has little or less taste. Change it to yellow and talk about lemons or citrus fruits, and the acid tastes of wine, for instance, suddenly become very clear. A red bundle of light allows them to experience much better and fruity tastes. Other colours give a negative result and can even let a good wine appear to be off.

Taste is, of course, always very subjective. Every individual is more or less susceptible to all these suggestive actions.

Later in this book we will deal with the dramaturgy of the enjoyment of smell and taste.

More experienced tasters will regularly want to exercise their skills by looking through the suggestions made.

In the practical applications we will quote some examples which the creativity of the chef can fully respond to. (See chapter 'Practical applications' p 68.)

> Why single malt whisky?

The inexhaustible supply of various aromas, only to be found in single malt whisky, makes us realize that there are no competitive products on the market for this application. Blended whisky has a far more one-sided palette of tastes and is therefore ruled out in any case.

Pure alcohol has even fewer results. This is because pure alcohol is almost without any taste and so has no added value to offer when it comes to adding extra tastes in the compilation of the desired result.

True connoisseurs and tasters already know that single malt whisky is an enrichment to our gastronomy. Whisky diners are here to stay, to say nothing of what the future can offer with these whisky-and-herbs aromas.

The purity of the spirit and its diversity of tastes open very many perspectives.

As well as simply tasting and enjoying the better whisky, there are many other options.

The choice of the right single malt for the right dish already gives added value, let alone when the taste of a dish has also been scented or enriched with the right malt whisky. No other drink in the world has such a diversity of tastes. And that is precisely why a single malt whisky is the obvious palatable basis for these applications, 'the extraction of aroma from spices and herbs'.

> What is whisky and what is single malt whisky?

All grain distillates that have matured in oak for the period of time laid down by law in the country concerned may be called whisky.

Grain distillates and malt distillates: from these two varieties the world production of about 3,700,000,000 litres of the finished product is made up. Scotland claims the lion's share. The reason for this is very simple. Scotland's abundant natural water reserves supplied the necessary source of energy for this. The drop in water where several watermills were built provided enough energy and power for milling and brewing. Later whisky distilleries were also built there.

Only malt whisky is subdivided regionally. Highland, Lowland, Midland, Speyside, Coastal and Island are the much discussed regions. However, this does not indicate more than the geographical location of the distillery. Personally I attach little importance to the regions, because whisky derives its taste mainly from the production and the maturation process.

Worldwide efforts have been made to approach the quality of the Scottish and Irish malt whiskies. Everywhere there are people hoping to lay their hands on some of the profits. Countries where the economy is still growing do not want this window of opportunity to pass them by. Disguised under the veil that this is done purely as a hobby or for fun, this is later always followed by commercial objectives.

Fortunately the authentic taste palette and character of malt whisky is still guaranteed.

The production of this whisky is unique and directed at quality.

In contrast to ordinary grain whisky, in which several kinds of grain are processed, barley is the only grain used in the single malt production process, with all the grain being malted. To put it briefly, this means that all barley grains are made wet. The moisture automatically starts a process of germination and growth. During this growing process enzymes are produced inside the grain which encourages the formation of sugar. At the right moment this process of germination is interrupted by drying the grain. Now we no longer talk about barley, but the grain is called malt, from which whisky has derived the name of malt whisky.

This grain is milled into a coarse flour known as grist. The grist is mixed with warm water to melt the sugars and in this way obtain a sweet liquid. Yeast is added to this sweet liquid, which converts the sugars into alcohol. This process we call the fermentation process. The result is called wash and is a kind of beer of about 8% vol. alcohol. From this beer the malt whisky producers distil the alcohol in copper distilling kettles, the pot stills (a kind of alembic).

The resulting spirit may only be called 'whisky' after the necessary number of years maturing in oak casks. The variety of oak casks used produces a treasury of varying results in taste and scent.

Every distillery is unique and aims for its own particular taste palette, resulting in the wide assortment of this product.

> The production of whisky and malt whisky in words and pictures: raw materials and taste enhancers

Water

Water is an indispensable source of energy in all known forms of life and civilizations.
In the production of whisky (comparable in some ways to brewing beer) water is monitored for composition, bacterial contamination, level of acidity and hardness.
The distilleries are located where there is plenty of naturally pure and soft water.

Grains

Barley, wheat, rye, maize. The quality of grain is indicated by a germination test and their weight per m^3 (based on the mass of the grain seed).

Yeasts

A diversity of dry and wet yeast cultures.

Peat

Peat is generally called the main taste enhancer of whisky. However, this statement only applies to a small part of whisky production. Part of the Scottish malt is lightly to heavily smoked with peat during the drying process, comparable to smoking fish or ham. The range of malts which results from this will consequently also have a taste palette varying from light to very heavily smoked. The most pronounced of them are given the nickname *peat monsters*, but they are certainly not appreciated by everyone.

Peat actually originates simply from the acidification of vegetable material.

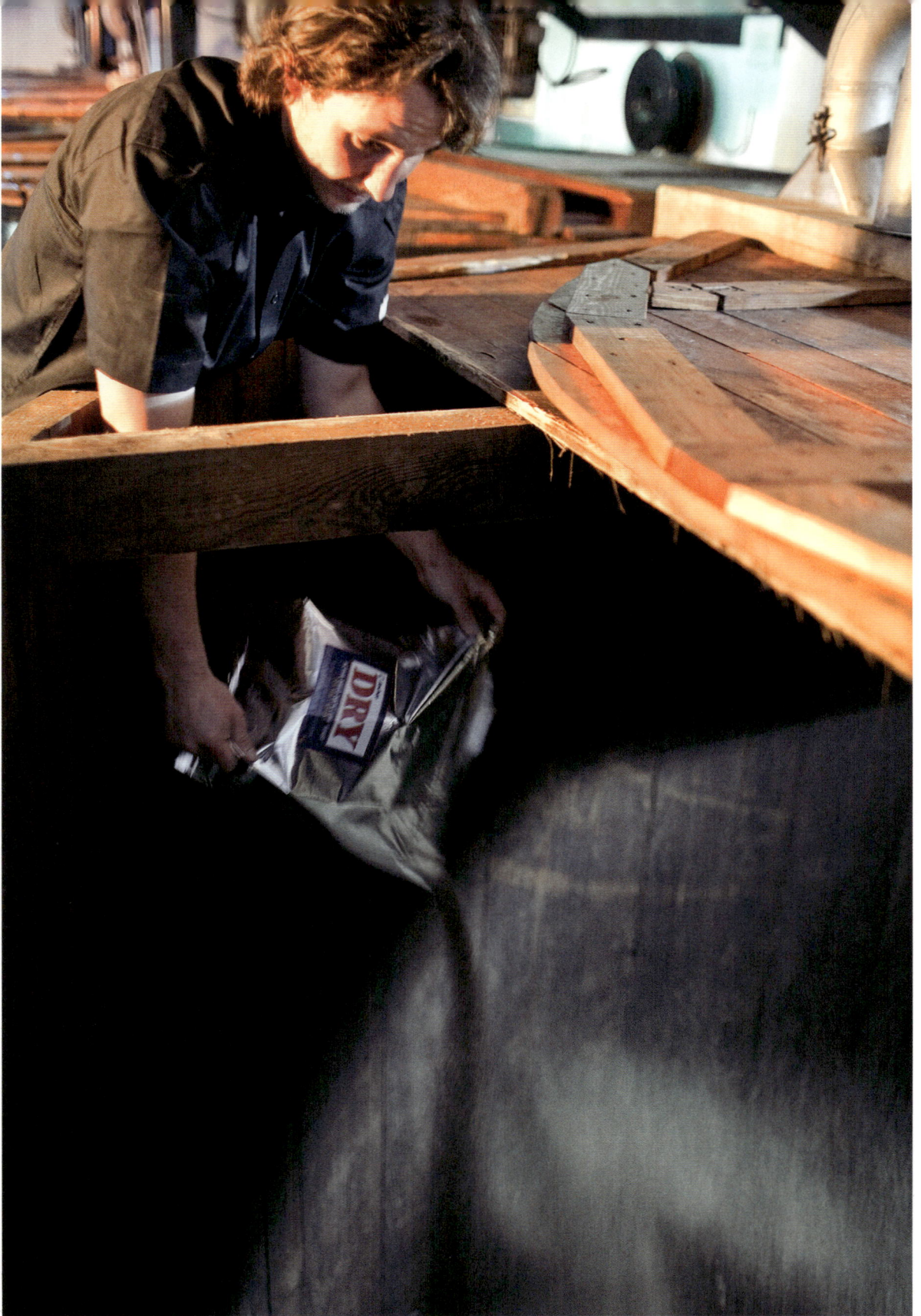

A fen or a lake can, for instance, change over the centuries into one large expanse of peat.

The mosses growing on the bottom of a lake can at some point suffer from a lack of air through their density, and consequently become acid. This process is repeated for thousands of years until the water area completely changes into an area of boggy stretches known as peat moors. Peat can also be the after-effect of a pile-up of small and large vegetation which as a result of natural disasters or climatological changes forms a layer on the surface. This is certainly not the precursor of coal, which is to be found deeper under the ground, where it turns into coal as a result of the greater pressure.

At the moment the peat is mainly reclaimed for horticulture (98%) and only 2% of the reclaimed peat is used for the whisky industry. At the current rate at which the surface is dug up, we should be able to carry on for another two hundred years. Meanwhile the use of peat as a fuel has almost completely ceased, whereas until recently even power stations made use of it.

Peat smoke is only harmful if people drink too much smoked malt whisky. PAHs (polycyclic aromatic hydrocarbons) are carcinogens which are present to a high degree in heavily smoked malts, but even then it would be more likely for someone to get a diseased liver from an excess of alcohol.

Wood

Since ancient times it has been known that there is a great variety in types of wood. Platters and drinking vessels have been made of wood since times immemorial. Yet not all kinds of wood are suitable for this. The same applies to maturing drinks in general and certainly to spirits which are inclined to have a very aggressive influence on the wood because of their high percentage of alcohol.

Casks are made and maintained by a cooper. The staves, together with bottom and top plates, are with a great deal of skill held together with the aid of metal rings.

Only oak is perfectly suited for the long-term maturation of spirits. The most commonly used sorts of oak are *Quercus alba* (North-American oak) and *Quercus robur* (native oak).

Wood has the property of rounding off the taste of spirits and letting them come to rest. Tannins which are present in wood and in almost all plants give off a bitter, dry and woody taste. New casks are rarely used for malt whisky. On the other hand, in the United States and Canada new casks are nearly always used, as is prescribed by law. To prevent too much taste of resin being absorbed from the wood into the spirit, the casks are generally singed inside with fire.

Ireland and Scotland use mainly used American whisky casks and Spanish sherry casks for storing whisky. Nowadays maturation often takes place in wine casks because the sherry casks are getting scarcer. This change will clearly alter the whisky landscape greatly in the near future. At the same time we will be offered a totally new range of variations.

> The production of grain distillates

Patent still

The first industrial whisky production has brought about a great change in the taste and finish of the product. In contrast to how it was done in the great breweries, the finish of the mash and wash was not directed so much at the clarity and the purity of this product, but aimed at the highest possible result in the conversion to alcohol. Distilling in a column distillation apparatus produced sometimes neutral, pure distillates, but also tasteless distillates, or even products with an unacceptable taste or smell, depending on the installation used. The presence of fusel oil and congeners (impure esters or acids) in too large quantities in these products made the improvement and enrichment of this product essential. Too many oil-like substances and insoluble small parts which are still to be found in these products after production, demand special treatment afterwards. Hence in the United States and Canada filtering through charcoal has provided a solution for several products to make the spirit more elegant and softer (mellowing).

Thanks to the continuous production all sources of starch are processed together or separately in a very productive way with a view to the most profitable result.
It is possible to go so far in making neutral distillates that they are sold as almost pure alcohol for further processing. For instance, in the Eastern Bloc countries the spirit is used for making vodka.

The process of this production can be compared to the production of malt whisky, if rather more industrialized. The different kinds of production are distinguished from each other by legal stipulations.
Rye has to be made with at least 51% rye and bourbon is made with at least 51% maize by law. 'Straight whisky' is not mixed with neutral distillates and is matured in accordance with the requirements of its variety. Sometimes singed casks are used for the maturation, and sometimes not.
Across the world many combinations are bottled in this continuous production process. Special and neutral distil-

lates have to give balance and fullness to the taste.
The addition of taste enhancers and colouring agents is not excluded in the world of whisky.

The term *sour mash* refers to the use of a *back set*, a residue from the distillation kettle, which can be added to the brewing kettle, the yeast vat or the yeast starter, and for some producers even all three. This has the advantage that there is better continuity in the taste and that the fermentation process is encouraged.

Malted Barley
Gemoute Gerst

Barley –
Gerst

Grist –
–
Gemalen
Gemoute Gerst

> The production of malt whisky

Malts

The production of malt whisky in comparison with the production of grain distillates is a craftsmanlike affair. The successive steps in this process are always carried out in minute detail and in the same way, and the same raw materials are always used to avoid creating differences in taste as much as possible. Selecting a quality barley is absolutely essential for a good start. Testing the barley seed is a must. Shape, specific gravity (as a measure of the presence of starch) and germinative capacity are checked. These days it is possible to buy barley anywhere in the world, with a satisfactory result; it certainly does not have to come from the country of the relevant production.

After a period of drying and rest, the barley seeds have to be activated again.

By allowing the barley to soak in water in large steeping tubs, the moisture level is brought up to scratch again. This triggers off a spontaneous reaction. Just as in natural circumstances the grain will want to propagate itself and therefore grows a germ which will root to make a new barley plant.

In the malt whisky production the dampened grains are spread out on a malt floor without soil, because as soon as it reaches the right phase, the barley seeds are dried to stop the growth of the plant. This procedure is known as floor malting, which is now rarely done (with a few exceptions, for instance for tourism). The industrial maltings which we also know from the world of brewing are more profitable.

This process of soaking, germination and drying is known as 'malting'.

Drying and whether or not to smoke (ppm)

To stop the sprouting process at the right moment it is necessary to remove the excess water from the seeds. This is known as drying or oasting. The kiln (or oasthouse) may or may not be equipped with a peat oven. To prevent all misunderstanding, we repeat that these days in most cases fuel oil or gas is used as a source of energy, and that peat is only used to smoke drying green malt. The number of hours taken and the intensity with which the peat smoke is sent through the layer of drying malt, determines the taste of smoke and peat which will be found in the final product, and which is expressed in ppm ('phenol parts per million'). While drying the temperature has to be watched carefully, because by drying too hot some substances might harden too fast with a less satisfactory result.

Milling

Although people talk about mills in the continuous production of whisky, it would be more correct to speak of crackers or cracking units in the malt distilleries.

It is essential to strip the load of malt or grain of dried roots or sprouts, and make them free of stones to protect the rollers.

The flour has to be milled to the correct fineness to achieve the desired result in the formation of sugar. The result is called grist.

Mashing and diastase activity

By adding warm water to the coarse grist, the enzymes which convert the remaining starch into processable sugars will be reactivated, and melting these sugars results in a sweet mash. This is normally done by means of three water rinses at three different temperatures to achieve the highest possible yield. The husk of the grain will serve as a filter and the sweet liquid will be pumped off to be processed further into a kind of alcoholic beer. The husks of the grain are known as 'draf' and are used as cattle fodder. By weighing the sweet liquid it is possible to measure the sugar content. The specific weight of liquids containing sugar is higher than that of pure water (which is 1,000 kg per m^3). In mash values of 1,050 kg per m^3 can be found in the first rinse water. With the second rinse these values go down. The third rinse contains so little sugar that it is no longer cost-effective, and can be used as the first rinse

water of the following run. The temperatures used are c. 60°C, 80°C and 95°C (variable for each distillery). In the brewery world as much protein as possible is usually broken down to achieve the clarity of the beer.

Wash or fermentation

This sweet liquid is subject to the necessary controls and tests. An optimal degree of acidity is needed and this can, if necessary, be adjusted. The message is to be on the look-out for bacterial contamination. Stainless steel is increasingly used instead of wood and copper in new installations or in renovating existing installations. Stainless steel is easier to clean and to maintain.

In addition yeasts are added to the sweet liquid, in solid or liquid form, depending on the equipment. These yeast cells immediately attack the sugars and convert them into alcohol and carbon dioxide.

The right temperature is carefully watched to maintain the ideal working climate for these yeast cells. The yeast cells will multiply themselves as long as they are nourished by the sugar in the right circumstances. According to the size of the washback, the quantity of sugar and the quantity of added yeast, this activity will take about 36 to 48 hours. Alcohol is lighter than water and this reduces the specific gravity, so that new measurements can determine what the result is. Non-convertible parts, water and alcohol together give a specific gravity of c.1,005 kg per m^3.

In the world of whisky a high degree of yeasting is usual, causing additional activity in the washbacks. The usual temperature for this to take place is 14 to 29°C.

As soon as all convertible sugars have been processed, the resulting 'beer' can be distilled.

Distilling

Alcohol has been distilled from as long ago as AD1000. The most important aspects have still not changed. The trade is still determined by the rule to achieve the correct alcohol and to remove the impure alcohol which is not suitable for consumption from the distillate. Ethyl alcohol or ethanol is the right component in spirit. But steps have to be taken to avoid that methyl alcohol or methanol find their way into the spirit. Again we can deduce from the specific gravity what the 'potential alcohol content' is. The distillate from the alembic or pot still is used in malt whisky. A copper alembic, also known as a wash still, is filled with the beer and this is brought to the boil. The specific gravity of alcohol is c. 800 kg per m³. The boiling point of pure alcohol is 78.3°C. The boiling point of wash is determined by the percentage of alcohol by volume still present. The alcohol present will easily come to the surface, boil and evaporate. In Scottish malt whisky production a double distillate is often used. Ireland, however, applies a triple distillate process.

An example follows here of the course of a run of a double distillate, in which nothing, or almost nothing, is lost. A wash still is filled with 15,000 litres beer. After distilling there is a loss of 9,300 litres, leaving 5,700 litres of low wines of c. 22% vol.
To these 5,700 litres the *feints* (top and tail) of the previous run is added, c. 3,260 litres at c. 36% vol. Together these make 8,960 litres at c. 28% vol.

These 8,960 litres are put in the spirit still and it is then distilled to produce the right amount of good alcohol. This is called the 'middle cut'. Approximately 4,000 litres are loss (water), c. 3,260 litres are again tops and tails (feints) and will be used for the next run. There will be c 1,700 litres at c. 70% vol left. After diluting it with water this will be put into the casks at c 63% vol. A good result is about 400 litres of spirit per 1,000 kg malt.

Maturation

The main purpose of the maturation of spirits is to give the product a richer, more balanced and fuller taste.

Grain distilleries pay a little less attention to the quality of the casks, but premium brands do not want to lose face. We will discover this in the quality.
It is also laid down by law who can and who may not use scorched casks. Hence the American 'straight corn' will always mature in non-scorched casks and 'straight rye' in scorched ones. Moreover, in the US and Canada most of these casks may only be used once.

On the other hand the malt distilleries can have a choice of various casks. There are already used American, Canadian, or sherry casks available on the market. In most cases these distilleries are part of international holdings. These holdings are in fact capable of working along established lines. Because within their own group they have Spanish sherry, American whiskey, Canadian whisky, Scottish and Irish production units, the exchange of casks is less of a problem. On the other hand there is an impending shortage of sherry casks to be borne in mind these days.

Maturation of a malt whisky always happens in the same selection of casks because it has an enormous influence on the eventual taste palette.

The supply of various types of sherry offers the master blender many possibilities. But as soon as a fixed style has been chosen, it has to be followed along the same lines Manzanilla, Fino, Amontillado, Palo Cortado, Oloroso and Pedro Ximénez are different types of sherry, each of which will add different tastes to the whisky. A combination of different sherry types, supplemented with American bourbon casks, is not exceptional.

The casks most used are the butt (500 l), cask & hogshead (250 l) and barrel (180 l). The name 'first fill' or 'fresh fill' is given to casks which are being used for the first time in malt whisky maturation after their use for sherry or other whisky. 'Refill' then refers to the second time these casks are used. From the third time onwards they have to be called 'plain oak'.

Dependent on the size of the cask there is a difference in the surface of wood and the contents of the cask. This means that whisky which matures in the same type of cask, but of a different size, will be a different product.

A large variety in finishes is the current picture. All sorts of casks are used to give a whisky an extra finish. Various wine casks, dessert wine casks, and casks which have served to mature a different strong drink, are filled for a period with already matured products. This gives these products an extra flavour or colour.

Filtering and bottling

Chill filtering (clarifying) is generally done everywhere. This is done to remove all non-soluble particles from the matured or unmatured products before bottling. For the consumer the clarity of a strong drink has always been a major factor in judging the quality of a product.
Adding colour with caramel to make the product look more attractive does not, in most cases, seriously affect the taste.
The tendency to filter consistently less and to retain the characteristics of the products has increased a great deal

in the last few years. Bottling at 46% vol because a great many fusels remain liquid at these high levels of alcohol has become standard practice.

Cask strength bottlings (and then mainly by independent whisky producers) are generally only filled into the bottles via paper filters. It is not exceptional for some of these products to become very cloudy when water is added (this happens less in *distillery* bottlings at cask strength). This will certainly not be the case with highly filtered products. Striving for diversity and uniqueness plays a great role here. And obviously not filtering or less thorough filtering also brings the production costs down.
In contrast to the wine-producing areas, which have had a type of bottle prescribed which would make the wine regionally recognized by that bottle, whisky may be bottled in all shapes and colours. Measures of capacity used to be a requirement, but this no longer needs to be observed. A bottling at lower than 40% vol alcohol may not be called whisky.
The label can contain a great deal of information about the product, but should not be considered as a reliable reference. The rule that 'what is not prohibited, is allowed' has inspired some very obscure descriptions on whisky labels. Whisky, blended, deluxe blend, pure, pure malt, malt, single malt, single cask, vintage, cask strength, single single malt, limited edition, dates and numbers, finishes and countries of origin are good and correct indications.
Descriptions such as 'rare', 'very old', 'special reserve' and so on are meaningless.

> Sniffing and tasting

The nose, once one of the most important organs of our body, is now used much less.
It used to determine our everyday behaviour. Odours alerted our curiosity and thanks to smells fresh food was found. Just like predators, primitive men used their nose for hunting and other urges.
Even an inexperienced nose can perceive smells in a way which cannot be equalled by modern technology.
Describing the aroma observed becomes constantly more difficult.

The dramaturgy of enjoyment

Just like the eyes, the nose is equipped with a kind of yellow spot, known as the nasal epithelium. The very sensitive olfactory cells send the smells they have observed to the brain. The analysis or naming of the odours observed, and whether or not they are recognized, depends mainly on the experience of the person involved.
With whisky, much more than with wine and beer, smell and taste are experienced together as a result of the strength of the product.

The assertion that the taste buds are completely nullified after tasting a third whisky and can taste no more is utter nonsense. The explanation can be found in the overlarge quantities of spirit which people swallow in one go. Rather can it be said that the taste buds are just beginning to become conditioned after tasting a third spirit. If the connoisseur in question does not want to be disturbed by the strength of the spirit, he can add more water to it, which is actually usual practice when describing whisky. This may and can if desired also be done when consuming it. It is recommended to taste no more than six spirits in a single session.

There is little point in diluting whisky to the strength of wine or beer; at most do it half and half. The supply of other drinks is so large that there are plenty of better choices available.

To find our personal preference there is a simple and amusing test. Serve the same distinctive malt in five identical glasses. Add different amounts of water to four of them: an equal quantity, half, a quarter and a teaspoonful In one glass you serve the pure whisky. Start with the glass containing most water and discover which quantity you prefer.

No manual is available about the exact way of going to work when tasting spirits. At the level of awarding medals and prizes in competitions you are completely dependent on the reputation and experience of the members of the jury.
So it is not surprising that enormous contradictions arise among them.

My personal experience shows that certain whisky products first need to be sniffed as thoroughly as possible before you start tasting and that others need to support the nose via the taste buds. Sniffing is actually also done to a limited, but certainly not unimportant, degree in the link between throat and nose, the nasopharinx. We call this indirect sniffing.
The same goes for the tastes, which are mainly experienced on the tongue, but which are also supplemented by the other areas of our nasal and tasting organs.

The mouth and nose are equipped with a taste and smell epithelium. The discerning cells are called the sensory cells. In the nasal epithelium these are located under the surface of the mucus layer. For the taste buds they are below in the folds of the taste pores. These sensory cells are connected to nerves which are bundled and form the link to the brain.

The glass that should be used is a very contentious subject. Too many firms see opportunities for profit in it.
All shapes and measures, with or without a lid, are now available on the market. Large balloon-shaped glasses in the shape of the familiar brandy glass give by far the best results. Of course, here too it is a matter of personal choice. The shape and attractive appearance also make up part

of the enjoyment. The experienced taster will make his own choice purely technically. Degustation is the conscious experience of smells and tastes.

Everyone will develop their personal tasting technique according to their own capability and experience.

Leaving spirits to stand for a little to develop bloom can certainly not do any harm. The right serving temperature and a room free of other smells are an absolute necessity.

Organizing a tasting is a job not to be underestimated. It is often necessary to do some preparatory work. Tasting beforehand, carrying out a few tests and if necessary making some changes, are all essential preparations. Contrasts that are too large cause products to lose out on the market and sometimes this is undeserved. A tasting organizer has to have the necessary know-how and experience. But as always: practice makes perfect.

Personally I like to taste and compare products of the same style.

For initiation tastings, however, there should be some noticeable contrasts, precisely because it concerns an initiation.

While tasting it is worth trying to recognize aromas and tastes from superficial to very intensive ones. It is usual to start by recognizing a specific taste pattern (primary tastes) and then unravel this further (the secondary tastes). For instance, you might recognize a fruity taste in the first place, secondly define it as a peach and thirdly place it as a dried or preserved fruit.

> The origin of tastes

'Primary' tastes come from the raw materials. Hence in malt whisky there will almost always be malt present in the taste palette. If it is a maize production a different starch gives it a different typical taste.

The 'secondary' tastes come from the production process. Here the selected temperatures, yeast cultures, water, size and shape of the brewing and stoking kettles will have a great influence on the result.

'Tertiary' tastes are formed during maturation. The chosen casks, sherry, madeira or port casks, casks previously used for other whisky, or even wine casks, will all one by one have a different influence on the spirit during the maturation period.

Analytical tasting or unravelling of the organoleptic elements after the production and maturation of a malt whisky is one step too far for some. Many continue to evaluate the finished products mainly on the richness of the tastes present, roundness, balance, and obviously, whether they like it personally. And that is in fact still the most important criterion for buying it.

> Practical applications

Unrivalled scenting of dishes

The technique of vaporizing whisky aromas has been used for many years. It is clear that the additional possibilities offered by these whisky-and-herb aromas, open up an ocean of applications.

Enriching dishes with whisky-and-herb aromas can be done just as well with a pipette. We then talk about sprinkling instead of vaporizing. If wanted this can be done straight onto the plate, next to the dishes, which can also have a useful function as a decoration.

Improved digestion of extracted aromas of certain fruits or vegetables which usually are difficult to digest.
For instance, paprika, garlic, dill and so on.

It will be possible to serve a single recipe, dish or roast with different flavours or even serve each guest at the dinner table their favourite aroma.

The speed with which the chef can season a number of different dishes to taste.

Being on a diet and yet enjoying tastes and aromas more intensely, just by using fewer fattening sauces and more whisky-and-herb aromas.

What and when

Usually dishes are seasoned to taste with these whisky aromas after they have been prepared.

Cold and hot dishes can be scented with a vaporizer or with a pipette.

Cold sauces of yoghurt, cheese, mascarpone and so on can be seasoned during their preparation.

A quick way of preparation is to crush herbs and spices in the mortar and mix them with the appropriate whisky. Apply this to the dishes with a brush or dip them into the extract.

Reducing, roasting or steaming with these aromas demands a little more experience. Although... practice makes perfect. The same goes for injecting roasts and poultry before preparing them.

Seasoning dishes, creating a vacuum and leaving the flavours to interact for a while.

Marinating and flambéing dishes can be done as in a normal cuisine, but give additional aromas from the herb extracts.

The theatre of senses:

As an example we show a best end of lamb, roasted and seasoned to taste by the chef and to his own choice. Just before serving you spray the upright bones of this roast with rosemary essence. The area round the plate is filled with extra aroma, without making the roast itself taste too strongly of rosemary. So we can enjoy more intensely with our nose without influencing the taste pattern.

Dishes which have been completely finished we can cover with domes and then spray the edge of the plate with extra aromas. Because of the volatility of whisky-and-herb aromas we again create perfect extra experiences for the nose without changing the taste of the dish.

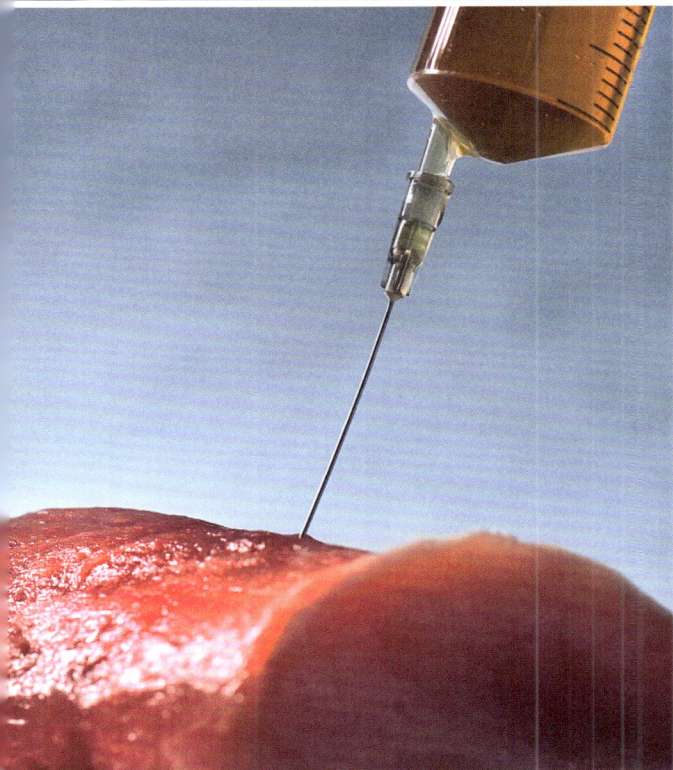

> Enjoying a serious diet

In fact we can clearly talk about a form of dieting here. By making use of whisky-and-herbs aromas on a regular basis, you avoid fattening sauces.
Without doubt unhealthy sauces put paid to a healthy diet. Moreover, you are seriously working with pure tastes. True connoisseurs can ask for nothing better. But beware, to my mind the message is that they should be offered as a change. After all, people like sauces. But then you should try out healthy sauces based on yoghurt with whisky-and-herbs aroma.

> Preparing single malt whisky aromas with fresh and/or dried herbs

In the next chapter there are forty dishes and applications with herbal aromas based on single malt whisky.
It is not difficult to make these yourself. The right proportions and a little bit of practice will make you realize very quickly that there is scope for a huge number of creations. For some herbs you may have to rely on whatever is available on the market. Sometimes a shortage of available fresh herbs means that you have to fall back on dried products. Experience will show that dried herbs can also have first-class results. Because of the alcohol dried herbs will give even more taste than when they are used in the usual way as a herb.

Crushing herbs and spices in a mortar can, when necessary, accelerate the preparation of an extract.

Opt by preference always for fresh herbs, because apart from the extracted products, a sprig of fresh herbs provides you with an attractive finish.

With the aid of this book everyone can make their own set of whisky-and-herb aromas. Your personal approach and choices, bearing in mind less digestible products, will be among the decisive criteria.

It is very important that you don't make unnecessary purchases. Remainders of fresh herbs you can dry or freeze. Leftover bought malt whisky will enrich your bar.

> List of often occurring spices, herbs and flavourings

Angelica	Garlic	Peppers
Anise	Ginger	Purslane
Basil	Horseradish	Rocket
Bay	Hyssop	Rosemary
Bergamot	Juniper	Rue
Borage	Lavender	Saffron
Camomile	Lemon	Sage
Caraway	Lemon balm	Salad burnet
Chervil	Lemongrass	Savory
Chilli peppers	Lovage	Saxifrage
Chives	Marigold	Sorrel
Cinnamon	Marjoram	Star anise
Cloves	Mint	Tarragon
Coriander	Orangeade	Thyme
Curry leaf	Oregano	Vanilla
Dill	Paprika	Verbena
Elderberry	Parsley	Water Milfoil
Fennel	Parsley, flat-leaved	

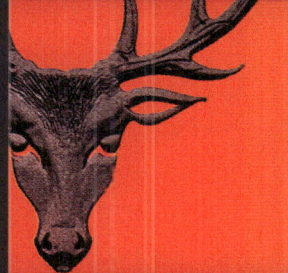

> List of malt whiskies, herbs and spices used

Malt whiskies and herbs described

An alternative of equal value

Auchentoshan 12 yrs	Mint	An Cnoc 12 yrs
Glenfarclas 10 yrs	Vanilla	Linkwood 15 yrs
Deanston 12 yrs	Saffron	Glenturret 10 yrs
Bunnahabhain 12 yrs	Star anise	Isle of Jura 10 yrs
Balblair 1997	Basil	Tomatin 12 yrs
Bruichladdich 2001	Chives	Arran 10 yrs
Balvenie 12 DW	Lemon leaf	Bladnoch 16 yrs
Old Pulteney 12 yrs	Dill	Scapa 14 yrs
Ben Nevis 10 yrs	Tarragon	Glen Garioch 12 yrs
Glengoyne 12 yrs	Curry leaf	Benromach 12 yrs
Talisker 10 yrs	Pepper mix	Springbank 10 yrs
Bowmore 12 yrs	Rosemary	Highland Park 12 yrs
Hibiki 12 yrs	Coriander	Glenmorangie 10 yrs
The Glenlivet 12 yrs	Sage	Glenrothes special reserve
Oban 14 yrs	Thyme	Dalwhinnie 15 yrs
Aberlour 10 yrs	Cinnamon	Macallan 12 yrs
Highland Park 12 yrs	Bay	Clynelish 14 yrs
Clynelish 14 yrs	Paprika	Bruichladdich 2000
Strathisla 12 yrs	Orange	Tomintoul 14 yrs
Dalmore 15 yrs	Juniper berry	Mortlach 15 yrs

A few aromas, to be prepared for various applications

Glenfiddich 12 yrs	Pepper mix	Bushmills 10 yrs
Glenmorangie 10 yrs	Chilli pepper	Glendronach 12 yrs
Glenfarclas 12 yrs	Pili-pili beans	Glencoe
Springbank 10 yrs	Cloves	Laphroaig 10 yrs (smoked version)
Tobermory 10 yrs	Garlic	Ardbeg 10 yrs (smoked version)

Cooking with whisky

PRACTICAL APPLICATIONS OF HERBS AND SPICES ON WHISKY

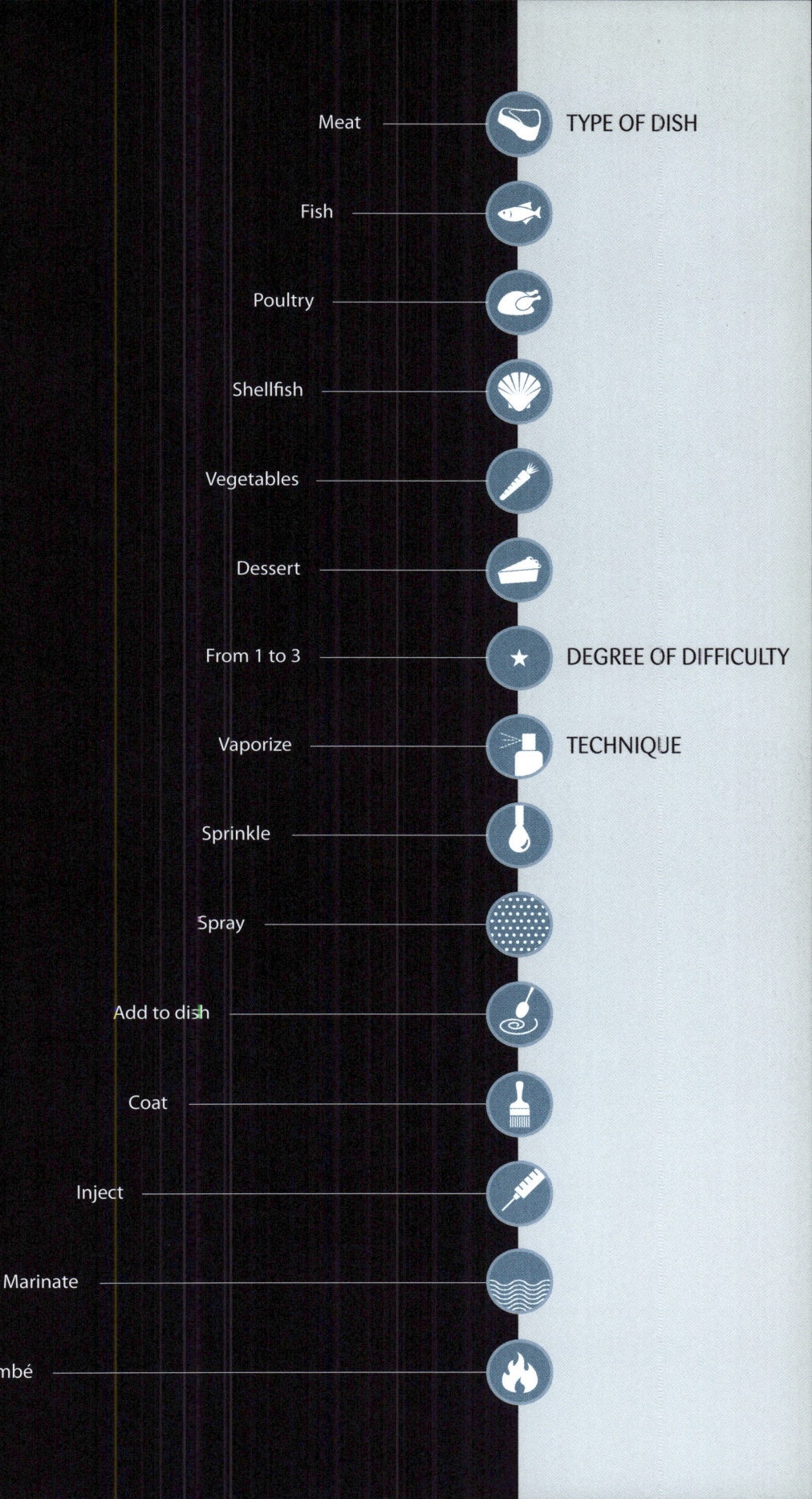

Meat — **TYPE OF DISH**

Fish

Poultry

Shellfish

Vegetables

Dessert

From 1 to 3 — **DEGREE OF DIFFICULTY**

Vaporize — **TECHNIQUE**

Sprinkle

Spray

Add to dish

Coat

Inject

Marinate

mbé

Mint

There are dozens of different kinds of mint, spread across more than half the globe. In green and moderate climates mint can be easily grown. From this supply garden mint and spearmint are most commonly used in our cuisine. Garden mint can be grown very easily in a small herb garden; it is a strong plant and gives out a restful aroma. While it is growing it is easy to check if the plant is ready for use. Rub some leaves between thumb and index finger and sniff, and you will know.

Applications:
Add a few leaves to tea (very common in most North-African countries), mint sauce (British cuisine), cocktails, salads, meat dishes and desserts, use it in pesto or in finishing off dishes. Fresh leaves, chopped small, dried and as an extract.
Health tip: it combats tiredness.

Auchentoshan classic single malt

Region: Scotland – Lowland Single malt. Environment of Glasgow, towards Loch Lomond.

Type: Mild, vanilla, citrus fruity, grassy, dries out gently. Perfectly suitable as an aperitif. In the nose a little more spicy with touches of grain and wood.

Mild mint flavours harmonize with the light touches of herbs and touches of wood.

Whisky-mint aroma:

Pick the leaves of 20 g fresh garden mint. Put these in a 10 cl bottle. Pour in Auchentoshan Classic single malt until the bottle is full. Seal and leave to infuse for three weeks. If desired you can remove the leaves and filter the whisky. Use a vaporizer or a pipette for applications in the kitchen.

Pea soup with whisky-mint aroma

Ingredients:

4 slices smoked ham
1 large potato (bintje)
1 onion, peeled
1 leek
butter
1 litre chicken stock
300 g frozen peas
100 g spinach
bouquet garni of parsley, mint,
chives and coriander
4 pieces toasted bread

Preparation:

Dry the ham for 2 hours in an oven at 60°C. Then grind it to a powder.
Peel the potato and divide it into pieces. Chop the onion.
Cut the leek into large pieces. Braise the leek and the onion in a knob of butter. Add the potato and the stock to it. Leave it all to cook for 15 minutes.
Add the peas, the spinach and the bouquet garni to the soup and leave it all
to cook for another 5 minutes. Remove the bouquet garni from the soup. Mix
the soup and pour it through a sieve. Season to taste with pepper and salt.
Vaporize the mint whisky into the soup bowl up to the top edge. Pour the
soup into the bowl and serve with the dried ham on a small piece of toasted
bread.

Whisky-mint aroma: Vaporize the whisky-mint aroma into the soup bowl or
cup up to the top edge, and preferably even a little along the outside.
As a bonus to the taste experience the whisky-mint aroma will, because of
the warmth of the bowl, add an extra dimension to the experience of aroma
and taste combined.

Mint tea bavarois with lemon meringue and lemon curd

Ingredients:

Mint-tea bavarois
2.5 dl water
1 bundle fresh spearmint
1 teabag mint tea
7 tablespoons sugar
1 vanilla pod
8 g leaves of gelatine
200 g quark of 0% fat

Lemon meringue
4 egg whites
1 teaspoon lemon juice
150 g sugar

Lemon curd
3 lemons
135 g sugar
2 eggs
165 g butter

Finish
fresh soft fruit
coconut biscuits

Preparation:

First make the mint tea bavarois. Heat the water and pour it over the fresh mint. Add the teabag of mint tea and leave to infuse for a few minutes. Pour the tea through a sieve and bring it to the boil with the sugar and the halved vanilla pod. Soak the gelatine leaves, dissolve them in the tea and leave the tea to cool. Stir in the quark and pour it all into a container 2 cm high. Put in the refrigerator for a few hours.

Next make the lemon meringue. Beat the egg whites, the lemon juice and the sugar stiff and spoon the mixture into a piping bag. Pipe balls of this mixture onto baking paper. Bake the meringues for 90 minutes in an oven at 90°C. Switch off the oven and leave the meringues for a little while to crispen up.

Meanwhile make the lemon curd. Wash the lemons and grate the rind (only the zest on the outside). Press 10 cl juice from the lemons.

Heat the lemon juice with the sugar and the zest until the sugar has dissolved. Stir the eggs loose in a pan. Pour the juice over the eggs and let it thicken while stirring continuously. (Take care! Don't let it boil!)

Add the butter and leave it to cool. Cover with baking paper, to avoid a skin forming on the curd.

When the bavarois has set, decorate it with the lemon meringues and fresh soft fruit on a strip of lemon curd. Finish off with a few splashes of lemon curd and crumbled coconut biscuits.

Whisky-mint aroma: Sprinkle it with a pipette on the bavarois.

Vanilla

Vanilla has become indispensable in our modern kitchen. There are very many applications possible with this flavouring. Vanilla is produced from an orchid which comes from Mexico and Madagascar. This plant is now cultivated in warm countries, mainly in Central America and Southern Europe. The fermented pods of this flower create the very characteristic vanilla flavour. As soon as the pod has ripened the inner part of the whole fruit (usually cut open), can be used in recipes.

As well as in food, vanilla is also much used in all kinds of scented oils, and even in tobacco.

Applications:

Rice pudding, pancakes, vanilla ice cream, desserts, sauces, and so on.

Boiled down in pudding and custard, sweetening with vanilla, in the modern kitchen to go with all kinds of meat dishes. As an aromatic oil vanilla has a bracing effect and it stimulates the appetite.

Glenfarclas single malt

Age: 10 years

Region: Scotland – Highland – Speyside near Aberlour

Type: Balanced and sweetish. Light touches of wood with caramel and vanilla. Fruity with mildly sweet smoky undertones. Harmonious nose with a medium long, pleasant aftertaste. In this whisky-vanilla aroma the sweeter hints of the whisky harmonize very easily with the vanilla. The light, fruity undertones finish it off.

Whisky-vanilla aroma:

Cut open four vanilla pods on the inner side. Take care that the pips are well exposed. Put the pods in a 20 cl bottle and fill it up with Glenfarclas 10 years old single malt. Add a sachet of vanilla sugar and leave to infuse. After three weeks it will be ready for use. There is no need to remove the vanilla pods.

Scallops with black pudding, smoked eel and apple

Ingredients:

1 Jonagold apple
1 black pudding
4 scallops
1 fillet of smoked eel
purslane

Vinaigrette
2 tablespoons apple vinegar
6 tablespoons corn oil

Preparation:

Cut the apple into a brunoise and fry the cubes crisp in a frying pan.
Make a vinaigrette of the vinegar and the oil and season it to taste with pepper and salt.
Cut the black pudding into four equal parts and cook them in the oven until done.
Fry the scallops briefly on high heat. Divide the smoked eel into four parts.
Arrange everything on the plate and use the purslane as decoration.

Tip: Finish off with a small ball of apple sorbet.

Whisky-vanilla aroma: Spray it over the dish.

Ham rolls with cambozola, fig chutney and almond biscuits with balsamic vinegar

Ingredients:

Fig chutney
200 g fresh figs
125 g apples type Renet
60 g onions
1 dl vinegar
1 teaspoon fennel seed
90 g caster sugar

Almond biscuits with balsamic vinegar
30 g unsalted butter
30 g crystal sugar
30 g flour
40 ml Liège syrup
1 teaspoon balsamic vinegar
30 g almond powder

Ham rolls with cambozola
4 thin slices of smoked ham
whisky-vanilla aroma
200 g cambozola
2 tablespoons nuts

Preparation:

Make the almond biscuits. Beat the butter and the sugar until it forms a ribbon. Mix the flour through it. Add the syrup and the vinegar. Lastly beat the almond powder into the dough. Make a thick roll of the dough and leave it to cool in the refrigerator. Cut the dough into biscuits of 3 mm thickness. Put the biscuits on baking paper and bake them in an oven at 180°C (about 6 to 8 minutes).
Arrange the slices of ham on foil. Spray it with sufficient whisky-vanilla aroma. Put the cheese on the ham and roll it up like a sausage. Put the rolls into the freezer for 20 minutes. Cut the rolls into slices and decorate them with nuts.

Tip: Use a few drops of balsamic vinegar as a coulis.

Whisky-vanilla aroma: Spray this during the preparation.

Saffron

The origin of saffron is disputed. Some people think it comes from China, others believe it is from the Middle East.

Saffron is in fact the stamen of the crocus, a lily-like flower which is now mainly grown in South-European countries. Saffron is very expensive because picking these flower stamens is very labour intensive and more than 200.000 stamens are needed for 1 kg of saffron.

Saffron is sold at varying levels of quality. This is because ground saffron is often mixed with other matter so that the taste varies.

By dissolving saffron in alcohol you can easily assess the quality on the basis of the residue left undissolved in the bottom of the glass.

The best way of buying saffron is as completely dried stamens, and to grind or crush these yourself. Apart from having a great deal of taste, saffron has a strong colour, which can make dishes look very attractive.

Applications:

Rice pudding, sauces, desserts, fruit dishes, meat, fish, poultry and game.

Deanston single malt

Age: 12 years

Region: Scotland – Highlands – Midland

Type: Lactic and sweet. Caramel, touches of sherry and slightly woody. Apple and toffee. Medium long finish connecting with aroma and taste.
Can simply be used as an everyday drink, as an aperitif and to accompany various dishes.
The lactic touches mix perfectly, as they do in desserts, with the pure saffron taste.

Whisky-saffron aroma:

Make this extract only in the quantity you need. The high price of pure saffron means that you can't afford to be lavish with it. One day before its use add the saffron you need to Deanston whisky. Sniff it after 2 hours of infusion and if necessary add a little more saffron to it. Be careful, because saffron has a very subtle smell and this is strengthened when spraying or using it in a dish. Use the aroma to smear over dishes, brush it on, dribble it on or spray it.

Paella with mussels, chicken and scampi

Ingredients:

1 kg mussels
white wine
pepper
mussel herbs
1 small onion
1 clove garlic
400 g rice
1 pinch of turmeric
1 pinch of paprika powder
chicken stock
400 g chicken ('Malines Cuckoo'
breed)
12 scampi
dried rosemary
whisky-saffron aroma
100 g peas
6 tomatoes
olive oil
garlic powder
pepper and salt
flat-leaved parsley

Preparation:

Rinse the mussels and put them into a large pan with a little wine. Add pepper and the mussel herbs to season it. Bring to the boil, cover, and simmer until they are done.

Sauté the chopped onion and the finely chopped garlic in olive oil and add the rice, the turmeric and the paprika powder.

Take the mussels off the heat and pour the cooking liquid onto the rice. Add a little chicken stock, cover and simmer till done.

Cut the chicken into strips and fry them briefly together with the scampi. Season with pepper, salt and dried rosemary. Spray them with the whisky-saffron aroma.

Blanch the peas briefly in salted water. Skin the tomatoes, cut them into a brunoise and braise them gently in olive oil. Season to taste with pepper, salt and garlic powder.

Take the rice off the heat and mix all ingredients together. Scatter a little parsley over it. Arrange everything on a plate. The number of mussels and the volume of this dish are dependent on its function: appetizer, first course or main course.

Whisky-saffron aroma: Spray the chicken and sprinkle the mussels.

Peach bavarois

Ingredients:

0.25 litre peach juice
3 tablespoons sugar
14 g gelatine leaves
2 tablespoons Balblair single
malt
0.2 litre lightly whipped single
cream
4 peaches
sugar
whisky-saffron aroma

Preparation:

Heat the peach juice with the sugar to just below boiling point. Soak the gelatine leaves and add them to the peach juice. Add the whisky and let it cool in the refrigerator for 20 minutes.

Stir the cream into the mixture and pour the bavarois into glasses. Leave to set in the refrigerator for 2 hours.

Cut the peaches into brunoise and fry the cubes in a pan. Scatter a little sugar over it and let them caramelize. Season with whisky-saffron aroma and leave them to cool.

Distribute the peach brunoise over the bavarois and finish off with a few fresh slices of peach.

Tip: You can add toasted almonds as a special finish.

Whisky-saffron aroma: Sprinkle the peaches.

Star anise

Star-shaped tree fruit from Asia. A very popular herb praised everywhere for its strong, pleasant taste and aroma.
The smell is reminiscent of liquorice or anise drinks.
The taste is very similar to our native aniseed, but is more intense.
You can use star anise dried and ground to a powder in a wide assortment of dishes.
It is used particularly in Oriental and French cuisine.

Applications:

In the kitchen, in all kinds of dishes, from soup, fish, shellfish, poultry and meat dishes to desserts.
You will also find it in cocktails and tea.
In short, it can't do everything, but it can do a great deal.
It stimulates the appetite.
You can use the dried fruits as a special decoration when making up the plates.

Bunnahabhain single malt

Age: 12 years

Region: Scotland – Isle of Islay

Type: Slightly smoky and toasted. Caramel, liquorice and very slightly smoked wood. Toffee with a few nuts. Medium length aftertaste connecting with aroma and taste.

A very balanced malt which can be served as an aperitif as well as with a variety of dishes. But shellfish and various fish dishes beat them all.
Very handy and with many uses in the kitchen.
The slight liquorice and toasted tastes harmonize with the star anise.

Whisky-star-anise aroma:

Take ten dried fruits. Put them in a glass bottle and fill it up with 20 cl Bunnahabhain single malt 12 years old. Leave to infuse for two weeks. The aroma may be filtered before use but does not have to be filtered.
This aroma can be kept a little longer. You can easily use it in a vaporizer for all kinds of dishes and appetizers. For various cocktails you can spray the glasses on the outside for an extra aroma without influencing the taste.

Spanish pork teamed up with celeriac

Ingredients:

Zest
1 tablespoon orange zest
3 tablespoons sugar
2 dl orange juice

600 g Spanish pork loin without bone

Sauce
2 tablespoons finely chopped shallots
1 teaspoon tomato puree
3 tablespoons Strathisla whisky
2 tablespoons orange juice
0.25 litre veal gravy
1 knob of butter
whisky-star anise aroma

8 tablespoons celeriac in brunoise
250 g French mushrooms
200 g celeriac puree (150 g celeriac and 50 g potatoes)

Preparation:

Boil down the orange zest with the sugar and the orange juice.
Divide the loin into equal parts. Seal the meat in the pan and then transfer it to the oven to finish cooking.
Meanwhile make the sauce. Braise the shallots in a pan. Add the tomato puree and deglaze with the whisky and the orange juice. Add the veal gravy and reduce the sauce to one third of the quantity. Add the zest and finish off with a knob of butter and the whisky-star anise aroma.
Stir-fry the brunoise of celeriac and mushrooms on a high heat. Reheat the celeriac puree in the microwave. Arrange everything on a plate and finish off with the zest and a few dried star anise fruits.

Whisky-star anise aroma: Add it to the sauce and spray the brunoise with it.

Grilled figs with red wine

Ingredients:

0.5 litre red wine
100 g sugar
1 cinnamon stick
black pepper
8 fresh figs
1 knob of butter
almond flakes
whisky-star anise aroma
2 spiced biscuits ('speculaas')

Preparation:

Bring the wine to the boil together with the sugar and the cinnamon stick and reduce it to half the quantity. Make the sauce spicy by adding a pinch of black pepper.

Cut the figs crosswise open to halfway. Arrange them in an oven dish and put a knob of butter on top of them. Leave them to cook in the oven for 4 to 5 minutes till done at 160°C.

Meanwhile toast the almond flakes.

Arrange one or two figs per person on a strip of red wine sauce and sprinkle them with whisky-star anise aroma with the aid of a pipette. Finish off with ground spiced biscuits and the roasted almond flakes.

Tip: Finish off with a ball of vanilla ice.

Whisky-star anise aroma: Sprinkle the fig with the aroma.

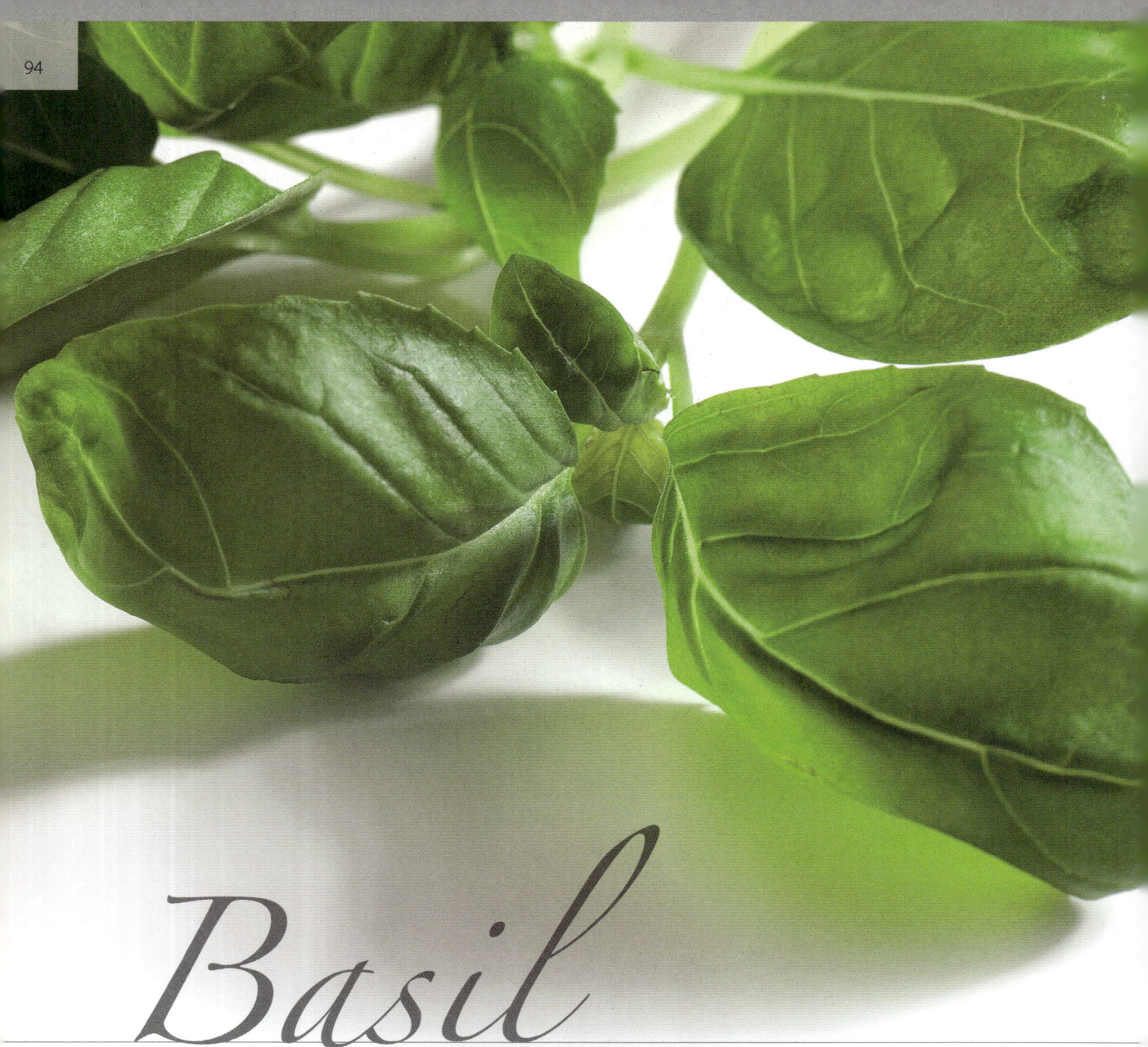

Basil

Basil is sometimes also known as 'the king's herb' in some countries. It is said that the name comes from the Greek 'basileus', meaning 'king'. It is easy to grow, outside or indoors in pots. Basil is used both fresh and dried. It has fresh green, aromatic leaves. Basil is mainly used to give dishes not only harmonious, but also subtle, yet strong accents. The taste is at its best if it is fresh when added. The medicinal properties of basil are mentioned in many herb books and it is used for a great diversity of complaints and diseases. The only thing I personally remember is that this herb should stimulate the memory card in our brain.

Preparations:

In soups, sauces, fish and shellfish, and in tomato dishes. But also in pasta dishes, and with veal, pork and lamb it is a first-class addition. The taste is subtle, but it can be recognized very easily. It should, however, not be combined with too many other herbs. Basil can also be frozen.

Balblair single malt

Age: vintage 1997

Region: Scotland – Northern Highlands

Type: Fruity (maturation in Fresh American Oak). Light exotic fruitiness reminiscent of melon and peach. Vanilla and caramel mingle into a balanced sweetness. Touches of wood float through accents of grain and malt. Chocolate with coconut filling. Soft, pleasant finish. Ideal as an aperitif and accompaniment to numerous appetizers. This malt whisky is also a perfect introduction to whisky for novices. The touches of fruit harmonize with the basil.

Whisky-basil aroma:

Fill a glass jar to the top with basil leaves. Pour on Balblair single malt until all the leaves have disappeared under the whisky. Close with a screw top and leave it to infuse for at least four weeks. With this aroma as extract you can scent dishes with a pipette or vaporizer. Use it to replace fresh basil, or in addition to it.

Tomato-prawns with garlic mayonnaise

Ingredients:

12 cherry tomatoes
200 g fresh, peeled prawns

Mayonnaise
1 egg yolk
1 teaspoon mustard
cornseed oil
whisky-basil aroma
2 cloves finely chopped garlic
pepper and salt

1 small radish
12 pieces sun-dried tomato
12 krupuk (prawn crackers)
12 balls of mozzarella
basil leaves

Preparation:

Scoop out the centre of the tomatoes and fill them with prawns.
Then make the mayonnaise. Beat the egg yolk with the mustard and pour in the oil slowly until you have reached the desired thickness. Season with pepper and salt. Add a few drops of whisky-basil aroma. Add the finely chopped garlic to bring it all up to taste.
Use a peeler to cut thin strips from the radish. Serve the tomatoes with the mayonnaise, and decorate with the strips of radish, the sun-dried tomatoes, the krupuk, the mozzarella balls and a few basil leaves.

Whisky-basil aroma: Add it to the mayonnaise and spray it over the dish.

Couscous with haddock

Ingredients:

Pesto
60 g basil
40 g Parmesan cheese
40 g pine nuts
1 clove garlic
olive oil

Couscous
1 chopped shallot
150 g couscous
1 dl white wine
2 dl chicken stock
400 g haddock in 4 portions
whisky-basil aroma
100 g lamb's ear herb
100 g samphire
butter
Parmesan flakes

Preparation:

Put all ingredients for the pesto, except the olive oil, in a food processor. Mix until you have a rough structure. Next add a fair quantity of olive oil and mix again.

Braise the chopped shallots in butter and add the couscous. Heat the white wine and the chicken stock and pour it over the couscous. Leave to swell for a few minutes.

Finish off with a part of the pesto.

Spray the haddock generously with whisky-basil aroma. Vacuum-pack the sprayed fish and leave it to infuse for a few hours. Alternatively you can also simply wrap the fish firmly in plastic foil. Remove the fish from the foil and dab it dry. Fry the fish crisp in a little butter in a non-stick pan and leave it till done in the oven for a few more minutes.

Blanch the lamb's ear herb and the samphire. Arrange the fish on the couscous and finish off with a strip of pesto and lamb's ear herb and samphire.

Tip: If you like it, you can also add a few Parmesan flakes.

Whisky-basil aroma: Spray the haddock with it and vacuum pack it.

Chives

There are several varieties of chives. The best known are the ordinary chives that can be found here everywhere. Oriental or Chinese chives taste and smell rather more like garlic.

The hollow, pipe-shaped leaves can give a strong herbal taste to food. But they are also very suitable as a decoration in the presentation of it.

It is one of the herbs which most people like to eat. For some it may be predominantly present, but for others preferably as subtle as possible. This is in fact more often the case with onion-type herbs.

Chives should not be confused with spring onions.

Applications:

Finely cut it is suitable for use in all kinds of salads and cold vegetable dishes.

Perfect as a finishing touch in soups and sauces. You can also use dried chives, but like many other herbs they will lose some taste.

Also used for garnishing the plate.

Bruichladdich 2001
classic single malt

Age: 10 years

Region: Scotland – Isle of Islay

Type: Coastal
Light lactic aroma with soft hints of soil or peat. Fresh, native fruit and citrus. Caramel and vanilla hints produce various sweet, candyish touches that continue into the aftertaste, which is balanced and pleasant. A light nutty taste rounds off this whisky. The slight taste of earth and peat blends with the chives.

Whisky-chives aroma:

Fill a glass bottle with the hollow leaves of chives. Put them in nice and straight so that as many as possible will fit into the bottle or jar. Next fill the bottle with Bruichladdich single malt 2001. Close with a screw top and leave it to infuse for at least four weeks. You can scent dishes with the aroma by using a pipette or vaporizer. You can also spray it on the outside of serving dishes to enhance the aroma.

Caesar salad 'with a difference'

Ingredients:

4 thick slices of white bread
olive oil
1 clove garlic
grated Parmesan cheese

Dressing
1 large egg
1 teaspoon Worcester sauce
2 tablespoons lemon juice
1 clove crushed garlic
4 anchovy fillets
1 teaspoon capers
1 teaspoon mustard
2 tablespoons whisky-chives
aroma
3 tablespoons cornseed oil

4 young herrings
1 granny smith apple
1 small onion
mesclun salad
4 slices bacon

Preparation:

Cut eight nice little sticks from the white bread. Spread them with olive oil and rub a halved clove of garlic over them. Scatter cheese over them and bake the bread golden brown in the oven.

Then make the dressing. Boil the egg for about 45 seconds and leave it to cool. Mix the Worcester sauce, the lemon juice, the garlic, the anchovy, the capers and the mustard in a bowl. Add the whisky-chives aroma. Beat the egg through it and stir it until you have a smooth mixture. Slowly add the cornseed oil while stirring constantly, until the dressing has the consistency you want.

Cut the herrings, the granny smith and the onion into brunoise and mix them with the dressing.

Arrange on the croutons. Finish off with the salad and the slices of bacon.

Whisky-chives aroma: Mix it into the dressing. Spray it as an extra aroma on the plate before arranging it.

Eel in chervil sauce

Ingredients:

1 bundle water cress
1 bundle flat-leaved parsley
1 bundle lemon balm
1 bundle coriander
1 bundle chives
1 bundle dill
1 bundle tarragon
salt
8 medium thick eels (skinned
and cleaned)
5 dl fish stock
3 slices of lemon
150 g spinach
250 g fresh garden sorrel
3 onions, chopped
pepper and salt

Preparation:

Rinse the herbs under running water and strip the leaves off the stalks.
Blanch the herbs briefly in salted water. Take them out of the pan, put them
in a blender and puree them.
Cut the eels into pieces and rinse them three times with salted water.
Braise the eel briefly and then pour on the fish stock. Add the slices of lemon
and simmer on low heat till the eel is done.
Take the eel out of the pan. Add the spinach, the sorrel and the onions to the
stock. Leave them to cook for a few minutes and mix it all. Next add the eel
again and the herb puree and season to taste with pepper and salt.
Arrange on a plate after the plate has been sprayed with the aroma.

Whisky-chives aroma: Spray the warm plate with the whisky-chives aroma
just before arranging the food and serve it quickly, so that the aroma of the
herbs is enhanced and the aroma spreads round the table.

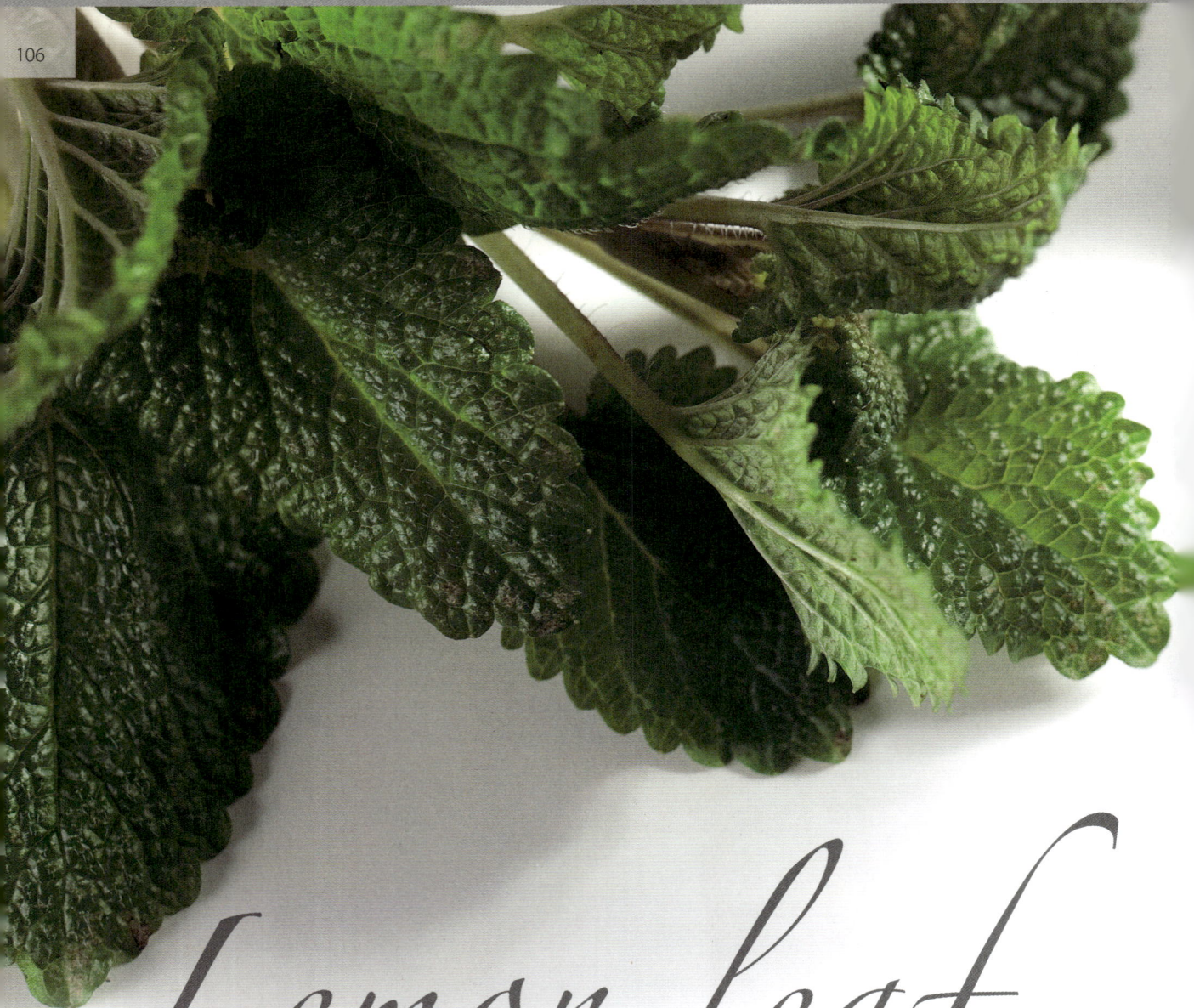

Lemon leaf

Lemon leaf comes from the Citrus hystrix (double leaf) and is often confused with lemon verbena. That does not really make much difference, because they are both suitable as citrus flavourings.

It has very aromatic leaves. You can cultivate it outside (in a moderate climate) and indoors. Lemon leaf is not hardy, you have to protect it against frost. You can, if you like, grow it in moveable plant pots. Lemon leaf is also a beautiful shrub. Pick the leaves you want to use fresh, and preferably pick young leaves.

Applications:

We meet lemon scents everywhere, in insecticides as well as in pleasant perfumes. And not least in the preparation of food. The diversity of lemon aromas is very large: there is lemon balm, lemongrass, lemon thyme and so on. The fresh, acid smell and taste are suitable as a finishing touch to very many dishes. You can use the aroma from starters to desserts, in cocktails and in tea.

Balvenie DW

Age: 12 years

Region: Scotland – Highlands – Speyside

Type: Sweetish and fruity. Caramel and toffee tastes mingle with a slight touch of honey. Touches of sherry with citrus and orange accents. Hints of chocolate and a rather sweet touch round off the taste. A very pleasant, rich aftertaste.
Generally praised and not only as an everyday drink. Comes out very strongly as an aperitif and to accompany various dishes.
The creamy, sweet touches also make this whisky a perfect accompaniment of desserts.
The slight hint of orange harmonizes perfectly with the citrus aroma.

Whisky-lemon leaf aroma:

Fill a glass jar or bottle with a wide neck with freshly picked lemon leaves. Next fill the jar or bottle with Balvenie DW single malt. Let it infuse for six weeks and then remove the leaves. Use a spray, pipette or brush to apply the aroma.

Vitello tonnato with capers and mustard salad

Ingredients:

3 dl dry white wine
3 dl chicken stock
thyme, bay, rosemary
600 g fillet of veal

Sauce
1 tin tuna
2 tablespoons capers
1 tablespoon sour gheurkins,
chopped into pieces
1 tablespoon lemon juice
mayonnaise

mustard salad
whisky-lemon leaf aroma

Preparation:

Bring the wine and the stock to the boil with the herbs. Put the veal into the stock and leave it on low heat for 25 minutes till done. Leave it to rest for 10 minutes in the cooking liquid, then remove the meat and leave it to cool in the refrigerator.
Next make the sauce. Mix the tuna with the capers, the gheurkins and the lemon juice in a food processor to a smooth mass. Stir a few tablespoons mayonnaise into it.
Carve the cold meat into thin slices and finish off with mustard salad, tuna mayonnaise and a few capers and gheurkins.
Spray with whisky-lemon leaf aroma.

Whisky-lemon leaf aroma: Spray with whisky-lemon leaf aroma.

Oysters with lemon leaf jelly and citrus cream

Ingredients:

12 oysters
1 tablespoon whisky-lemon leaf aroma
1 dl dry white wine
2 leaves of gelatine
pepper

Citrus cream
3 tablespoons cream
1 tablespoon lemon juice
1 tablespoon whisky-lemon leaf aroma
pepper

lemon zest

Preparation:

Open the oysters and catch the juice. Heat the whisky-lemon leaf aroma with the white wine and the oyster juice. Soak the leaves of gelatine, stir them into the liquid and leave this to cool and set.
Scatter a little freshly ground pepper on the oysters.
Next make the citrus cream. Beat the cream, the lemon juice and the whisky-lemon leaf aroma gently with a fork. Season with pepper.
Arrange the oysters on a plate and finish off with finely cut jelly and the citrus cream.
Decorate with a small pinch of grated lemon zest. Only use the thin outer skin.

Whisky-lemon leaf aroma: Use the aroma in the jelly and the citrus cream. The oyster can be sprayed a little more for those who like that.

Dill

A herb shelf without dill is almost unthinkable. Dill is also present everywhere in our herb gardens. The plant is hardy, but a sunny position is important. You can use the leaves as well as the seeds of dill. Because of the many kinds of applications it is advisable to sow dill over a period of time, so that you have a constant supply of fresh herbs. You can also freeze or dry sprigs you have cut, so that you have a ready supply in the winter too. But like so many other herbs fresh dill is available throughout the year in the stores.

Preparations:
Dill is probably the most commonly used herb in the preparation of fish dishes.
You can also use it in salads and preserved vegetables, for cold sauces and fresh or dried with hot dishes.
It is also suitable for marinades.

Old Pulteney

Age: 12 years

Region: Scotland – Northern Highlands

Type: Fruity and mild. Apple and caramel with a slight hint of liquorice. Fruity taste which evolves into sweets. Light touch of chocolate towards the end. Very round, pleasant aftertaste.
A whisky with a great deal of potential to please a wide public. Because of the soft, salty-sweet touches this whisky is the perfect companion to various fish dishes and much more. The mild dill aroma fits into the picture.

Whisky-dill aroma:

Cut enough fresh dill and remove the thick stems. Put a small twig of fresh parsley on the bottom of a glass jar or bottle. Fill up with fresh dill until the jar is quite full. Add Old Pulteney single malt to it. Close the jar and leave the contents to infuse for at least six weeks. Spray the aroma, use a pipette or simply add some.

Gravadlax

Ingredients:

400 g salmon fillet
whisky-dill aroma
100 g salt
120 g sugar
2 slices bread

Dill dressing
3 tablespoons plain yoghurt
2 tablespoons mayonnaise
2 tablespoons dill

1 cucumber

Preparation:

Rub the salmon with the whisky-dill aroma and let it rest for 10 minutes.
Mix the salt and the sugar and rub the salmon with this mixture. Vacuum-pack the fish and leave it to rest in a cool place for two days. Remove the salmon from the vacuum pack and cut it into cubes.
With a round or other form cut out shapes from the bread and fry them in a pan until they are crisp.
Next make a dill dressing. Mix the yoghurt, the mayonnaise and the dill and season them to taste with pepper and salt.
Cut the cucumber into pieces and scoop out the centres so that a cylinder of thin peel remains. Fill these with the salmon cubes. Finish off with the dressing and the bread. Use a little fresh dill for decoration.

Whisky-dill aroma: Rub the salmon in with the extract and vacuum pack it. Spray the bread when arranging the plates.

Smoked trout with cucumber

Ingredients:

1 smoked trout fillet
1.5 cucumber
1 teaspoon finely chopped dill
1 teaspoon chopped onion
2 tablespoons dill
vinegar
pepper and salt
1 gelatine leaf
75 g cream of 8% fat content
syphon with N_2O capsule
whisky-dill aroma

Preparation:

Cut the trout and half a cucumber to a fine brunoise. Mix this with the finely cut dill and the chopped onion.

Mix the rest of the cucumber and the uncut dill in a blender and season to taste with vinegar, pepper and salt. Strain this liquid through a conical strainer.

Heat 70 ml of the liquid. Soak the gelatine leaf and then add it to the warm liquid. Stir until it has dissolved and then add the liquid to the rest of the cold cucumber liquid (approximately 150 ml). Pour this together with the cream into the syphon. Leave to cool in the refrigerator.

Just before arranging and serving the meal put the syphon under pressure with an N_2O-capsule. Spray the serving glasses on the inside with the whisky-dill aroma. Next spoon the trout and cucumber brunoise into the glasses. Spray with the whisky-dill aroma and finish off with the foam.

Whisky-dill aroma: Spray the glasses and sprinkle on the dish.

Tarragon

Apparently the tarragon herb only appeared in our cuisine a few centuries ago. In Asia it was known a little earlier, more exactly in the Middle Ages.

Tarragon has a very characteristic taste. Many associate this taste with liquorice or anise. It is one of those flavours which people either like or totally dislike. The plant exists in various varieties and is usually not hardy. It needs some protection against too much water, and a great deal of sun. Tarragon can also be grown perfectly well in pots. It is a fantastic taste enhancer fresh or dried, and it can be combined with many other herbs and spices.

Applications:

Best known is béarnaise sauce. But you can also scent salads and various meat and fish dishes with this herb. Marinate, vaporize and sprinkle, all are possible.

Ben Nevis

Age: 10 years

Region: Scotland – Highlands

Type: Sweetish, fruity. Caramel with touches of various nuts. Slightly lactic. Sweetish with a fruity undertone. Slight hints of chocolate towards the ends. Strong aftertaste with expanding tastes.
Reasonably approachable whisky despite its strength. Perfect accompaniment to various meat and cheese dishes. The sweet touches merge extremely well with the tarragon extract.

Whisky-tarragon aroma:

Tarragon clearly needs a little more time than many other herbs. You have to fill the jar or bottle really full with the herb and fill up with the Ben Nevis malt. You can safely leave it to infuse for two to three months, depending on the aromatic strength of the plants.
If you don't make too much and use the aroma regularly, you don't need to remove the leaves.

Gambas with béarnaise sauce

Ingredients:

4 gambas (large prawns)
garlic powder
pepper and salt
2 slices of braised bacon 1 cm
thick
whisky-tarragon aroma
250 g oyster mushrooms

Béarnaise sauce
150 g butter
2 egg yolks
1/2 lemon
2 tablespoons whisky-tarragon
aroma
salt
cayenne pepper
1 tablespoon freshly cut
tarragon

Preparation:

Take the gambas out of their shells and remove their intestines. Fry them on high heat and season them with garlic powder, pepper and salt.

Cut the slices of bacon in half and put them in the oven till done. Inject the bacon with the whisky-tarragon aroma.

Fry the oyster mushrooms briefly at a high heat. Season them with garlic powder, pepper and salt.

Next make the béarnaise sauce. Melt the butter in a small bowl and remove the milk deposits.

Beat the egg yolks with the juice of half a lemon and the whisky-tarragon aroma on a low heat to a firm foam. Stir the clarified butter carefully into the sabayon until a smooth sauce if formed. Season to taste with salt, a pinch of cayenne pepper and the fresh tarragon.

Arrange first the oyster mushrooms on the plate and cover them with the bacon. Finish off with the gambas and the béarnaise sauce.

Whisky-tarragon aroma: Inject the aroma into the bacon and use it in the béarnaise sauce.

Bass with asparagus

Ingredients:

12 asparagus
salt
4 bass fillets with skin
olive oil
pepper

Butter sauce
1 shallot
1 tablespoon capers
2 tablespoon whisky-tarragon
aroma
1 dl fish stock
150 g butter

Finish
Whisky-tarragon aroma
mix of dried fish herbs
fresh tarragon

Preparation:

Peel the asparagus and cook them al dente in lightly salted water.
Cut the bass fillets in two equal parts and fry them in olive oil with the skin side down. Season them with pepper and salt and put them in the oven at 200°C for 5 minutes till done.
Next make the butter sauce. Chop the shallot finely and braise them together with the capers. Add the whisky-tarragon aroma and the fish stock and bring to the boil. Next put the stock on a low heat and slowly melt the butter into it.
Spray the plate with tarragon aroma before arranging the food. Place the bass and the asparagus on the plate and finish off with the sauce, dried herbs and fresh tarragon.

Whisky-tarragon aroma: Spray the plate with it and use the aroma in the sauce.

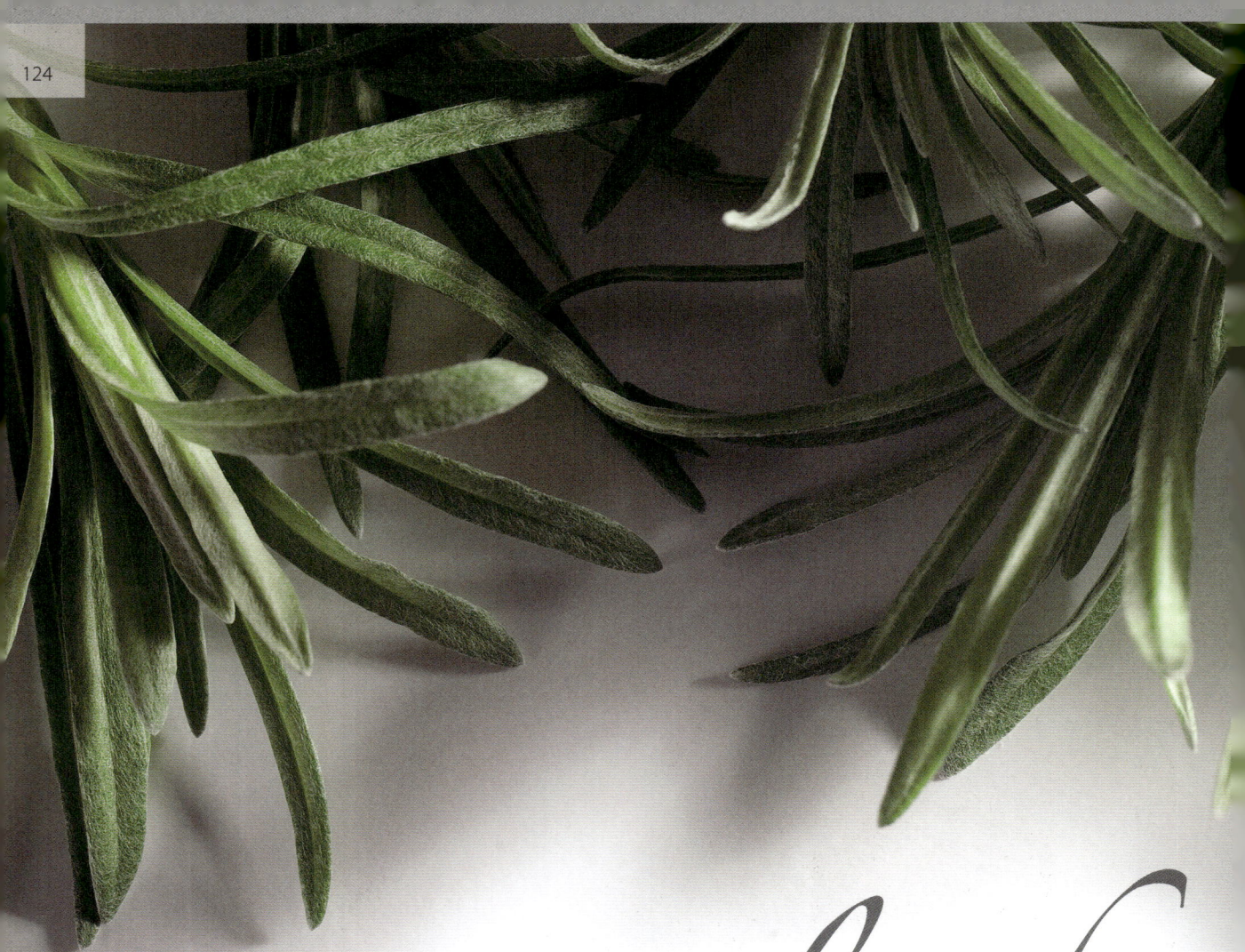

Curry leaf

Curry leaf looks like the familiar rosemary but it tastes and smells quite different. It clearly comes from the oriental cuisine, but should not be confused with curry powder, which is usually a mixture of different herbs and spices, fortified by chilli peppers. Curry leaf is difficult to grow in our climate. It needs a great deal of warmth. In the past it could only be found in oriental food shops; now it is to be found in all outlets selling herbs and spices, but then in dried form.

Preparations:
The leaf can be used in cooking various stews and dishes. You can also use it for ready-made dishes and as a ground dried herb. You can use it in marinades. To my mind it is too easily reserved for use in oriental dishes and in combination with other oriental herbs and spices.

Glengoyne

Age: 12 years

Region: Scotland – Central Highlands

Type: Soft and approachable. Hints of maturation in bourbon cask and sherry cask. There are touches of both fruit and sweets to be found in this whisky. Slight tastes of wood and nut take care of the balance with vanilla and caramel. A nice soft after-taste with light touches of nuts.
An introductory whisky but also nice as an everyday drink. Neither meat, fish and cheese dishes will eschew this whisky. The balanced touches of wood in this whisky allow the curry leaf aromas to blend perfectly into the whole.

Whisky-curry leaf aroma:

Plan making this extract or aroma long enough in advance. Fill a glass jar full of the dried leaves, preferably without breaking the leaves. You can leave it to infuse for one to four months. It clearly becomes more intense if left for a longer period, but it does lose its freshness a little. Smell and taste it regularly. If necessary you can remove the leaves when the desired result has been achieved.

A chicken casserole with a difference

Ingredients:

4 shallots
5 carrots
whisky-curry leaf aroma
1 piece of leek
1 stick celery
thyme, bay leaf
1/2 lemon
1 litre chicken stock
4 chicken fillets

Sauce
30 g flour
30 g butter
1/2 litre hot stock
1/2 litre low-fat soya milk
2 egg yolks
1.5 dl low-fat cream
2 tablespoons chopped parsley

250 g beech mushrooms
(shimaji)
1 leek
12 pearl onions

Preparation:

Put the shallots, two of the carrots, the whisky-curry leaf aroma, the leek, the celery, thyme, bay and the lemon juice in the stock and cook the chicken fillets until they are almost done. Remove them from the stock, dab them dry, inject them with the whisky-curry leaf aroma and fry them crisp in a very hot pan.

Then make the sauce. Make a roux with the flour and the butter. Add the hot stock and the soya milk. Allow it to thicken. Meanwhile mix the egg yolks and the cream and add them in the end to bind the sauce. Finish off with parsley.

Cook the remainder of the carrots until done and puree them. Take the stalks off the mushrooms and fry them on a high heat. Cut the leek into a fine julienne and deep-fry these till crisp at 180°C. Remove the skins from the pearl onions and braise them.

Spray the plate with the whisky-curry leaf aroma and pipe the carrot puree into a lovely trail. Put the chicken on top of the puree, pour the sauce over it and finish off with the deep-fried leek. Finish the decoration with the beech mushrooms and the pearl onions.

Whisky-curry leaf aroma: Spray the plate with it and inject the chicken with the aroma

Lobster with a curry dressing

Ingredients:

1 lobster, approx. 700 g
court bouillon
2 tablespoons vinegar
1 Granny Smith apple
whisky-curry leaf aroma
4 cauliflower florets
turmeric
salt
4 long strands of cucumber

Dressing
2 tablespoons mayonnaise
3 tablespoons yoghurt
black pepper
sea salt
curry powder

fine curly lettuce
4 tablespoons walnut oil
2 tablespoons white balsamic
vinegar

Preparation:

Cook the lobster in the court bouillon to which you add vinegar. Let it cool and remove the lobster meat from the shell. Cut it small.

Peel the apple and cut it in a fine brunoise. Marinate the cubes of apple with whisky-curry leaf aroma.

Blanch the cauliflower florets for 2 minutes in water to which you add turmeric and salt. Next mix the cauliflower till fine in a blender.

Mix all previous ingredients (keeping back a few cubes of apple and pieces of lobster for garnishing) and push them well down into small moulds. Take them out of the moulds and wrap a strip of cucumber round each shape.

Next make the dressing. Mix the mayonnaise with the yoghurt and season to taste with black pepper, sea salt and curry powder.

Spoon a little dressing on the plates. Place the cucumber-wrapped lobster mixture on the dressing. Finish off with the fine curly lettuce. Mix the oil with the vinegar and pour the mixture over the lettuce. Garnish as you like with the leftover pieces of apple and lobster.

Whisky-curry leaf aroma: Marinate the apple with it.

Pepper mix

The supply of peppers is so great and there are so many different varieties, that we could in fact have written a book on peppers alone. Who isn't aware of the picture of a North-African, oriental or Arabian market where dozens of different ground and fresh peppers are being sold. The tastes vary from highly explosive to mildly warming. Many a peppermill takes care of the finishing touch in seasoning many dishes. Dried peppercorns come from tropical countries. The colour is the result of picking unripe or ripe fruits. When you know that people have fought wars for the sake of peppers, you realize how important pepper is.

Applications:

It is impossible to think of our cuisine without pepper. It is the most important taste enhancer next to salt. Nearly every meal has something that needs pepper. It is striking that for some its presence may be very strong, while others prefer it more subtle. The provision of freshly ground peppercorns alongside a vaporizer with the extract is very simple and can be used perfectly according to personal taste and dosage. You can use pepper in marinades. Spray or sprinkle it on salads and meat (steak au poivre), fish dishes and vegetables, in soups and potato dishes.

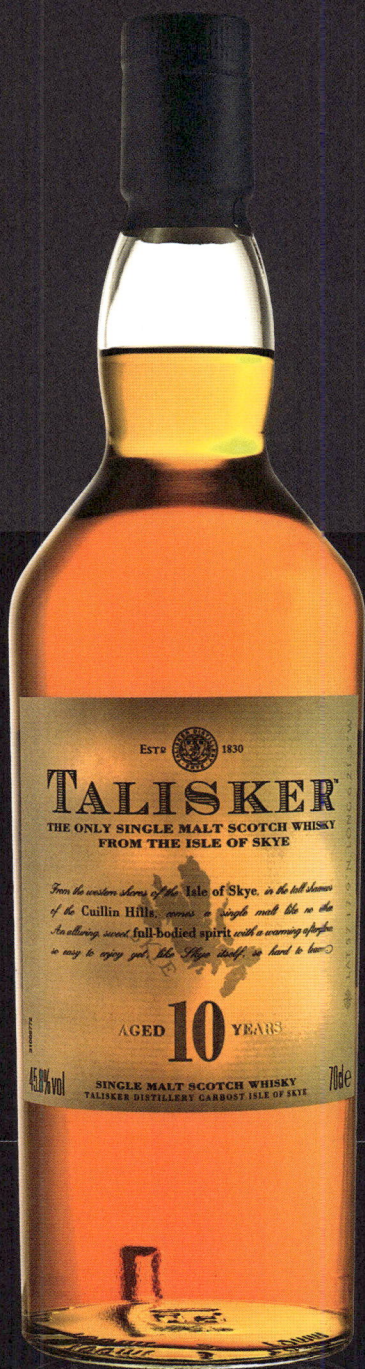

Talisker

Age: 10 years

Region: Scotland – Isle of Skye

Type: Smoky. Intensely full-tasting Island whisky. Medium peat-smoked with strong hints of herbs. The sweet, candy-like touch ensures a balance. Smoke, salty with hints of the sea give this whisky its specific character. A slight medicinal taste which is certainly not intrusive, mingles with the preceding qualities and gives a fine, long aftertaste. A rich whisky, praised everywhere, despite its strength. Its harmony with pepper is evicent from the presence of the spicy hint of pepper in this whisky.

Whisky-pepper mix aroma:

Fill one third of a glass bottle or jar with a mix (black, red, white etc.) of peppercorns. Fill the bottle up with Talisker single malt. Next add a chilli pepper which has been cut into pieces. After three to four weeks the aroma will be ready for use. You can keep it for a long time. Don't be afraid to experiment with different kinds of pepper.

Parcel of ostrich fillet with pear and cheeses

Ingredients:

400 g ostrich fillet
1 conference pear
1 lemon
2 slices smoked ham
100 g ricotta cheese
50 g soft Hinkelspel cheese
(type Roquefort)
pepper and salt

Dressing
1/3 raspberry vinegar
2/3 olive oil
pepper and salt

blue cheese
a few leaves of rocket and herbs
whisky-pepper- mix aroma
a few peppercorns

Preparation:

Put the ostrich fillet in the freezer for 20 minutes, so that you can easily carve wafer-thin slices of meat from it.
Cut the pear in brunoise and sprinkle it with a little freshly pressed lemon juice. Cut the smoked ham into a fine julienne. Mix the ricotta with the cheese from the Belgian cheesemaker Het Hinkelspel. Add the pear and the ham to the cheese mixture. Season to taste with pepper and salt.
Put the wafer-thin slices of ostrich on baking paper and put a spoonful of the cheese mixture on it. Fold the meat round the cheese mixture.
Make a dressing of the vinegar and the olive oil. Season to taste with pepper and salt.
Arrange the blue-veined cheese on a plate first. Place the ostrich-and-cheese parcel on top of it. Decorate with rocket, a few pieces of pear and green herbs. Spray the cheese parcel with the whisky-pepper mix aroma. Finish off with the dressing and a few pepper corns.

Whisky-pepper mix aroma: Spray the ostrich-and-cheese parcel.

Beef fillet with a tomato carpaccio

Ingredients:

4 fillets of beef (about 150 g)
from Belgian Blue-White cattle
8 strips of Breydel bacon

Sauce
1 small onion
2 teaspoons dark brown sugar
3 tablespoons dark Augustijn
beer
1 dl veal gravy
1 tablespoon balsamic vinegar

Beer dough
1 egg
3 dl beer
200 g flour

2 tomatoes
whisky-pepper mix aroma
400 g spinach
8 onion rings
2 large baking potatoes
peppercorns
a few leaves purple shiso
1 spring onion

Preparation:

Wrap the bacon round the fillet of beef. Sear it in a hot pan and then transfer it to the oven till done.

Next make the sauce. Braise the finely chopped onion in a pan and add the dark brown sugar to it. Deglaze it with the dark Augustijn beer and add the veal gravy to it. Reduce by 1/3 and season with the balsamic vinegar.

Cut the tomatoes into thin slices and spray them with the whisky-pepper mix aroma. Heat them in the oven. Braise the spinach in the pan and keep it warm. For the beer dough beat the egg into the three dl beer. Mix the flour in until you have no more lumps. Dip the onion rings into the beer sauce and deep-fry them at 180°C.

Peel the potatoes and cut them into thin slices. Deep-fry them at 180°C. Take the meat out of the oven and brush it with whisky-pepper mix aroma. Place the spinach on some of the sauce with the aid of a small mould. Put a layer of tomato on top of this. Put the meat on top of the tomato and finish the arrangement with the onion rings, the potato chips, peppercorns, the purple shiso and the spring onion.

Whisky-pepper aroma: Spray the tomato and brush the meat with it.

Rosemary

Without doubt the smell of rosemary is as important, perhaps even more important than the taste. The aroma is experienced as one of the nicest scents in the world of herbs. It is an easy to grow, hardy plant. It can be grown in pots indoors as well as in the open outside.

Rosemary comes for the Mediterranean area and obviously grows best in warm climates. It is difficult to imagine any cuisine in the world without this herb. It is said that rosemary has a whole range of medicinal properties. You will be able to find them in various herbals.

Applications:

Rosemary can be a taste enhancer for anything from an appetizer to a dessert. It is often used in combination with a large number of other herbs. In meat dishes, fish, game, sauces and salads. Fresh, ground or in marinades, in outdoor cooking and barbecue meals. Thyme and garlic are true companions of rosemary.

Bowmore single malt

Age: 12 years

Region: Scotland – Isle of Islay

Type: medium peat-smoked. Hints of caramel and mild smoke mix with floral scents. The pleasant taste of peat is completely balanced by a salty hint of the sea. Among the sweet tastes there is, alongside caramel, a hint of chocolate. There are undertones of fruit. A strong, long aftertaste with hints of violet and iocine. For those who don't like their malt whisky to be too heavily peat-smoked, an older version, for instance 15 years old, may be the answer. The strong taste of rosemary will find a worthy complement in Bowmore single malt.

Whisky-rosemary aroma:

Preparing this aroma is just as simple as all previous ones. A little imagination and creativity on the part of the chef is welcome. Fill a small bottle or jar well with fresh rosemary and fill up with Bowmore single malt. You can make up various compositions one with a little thyme or even a small clove of garlic, another with basil or pepper. You can safely extract various combinations of rosemary aromas. Leave them to infuse for at least three to four weeks and make a fresh aroma at regular intervals.

Hamburger of lamb with parsnips and paprika ketchup

Ingredients:

2 slices of white bread without crust
3 tablespoons Clynelish whisky
600 g minced lamb
2 tablespoons finely chopped shallot
1 clove garlic
1 egg
pepper and salt
curry powder
2 parsnips

Paprika ketchup
1 finely chopped onion
750 g tomatoes
2 red paprikas
1.5 dl apple vinegar
1 teaspoon mustard
40 g sugar
1 tablespoon ketchup
whisky-bay leaf aroma

Garlic dressing
1 clove of garlic
1 tablespoon yoghurt
2 tablespoons mayonnaise
pepper and salt

1 courgette
3 paprika's: red, green and yellow
whisky-bay leaf aroma

Preparation:

Soak the bread in the whisky for a few minutes. Knead the mince with the shallot, the crushed garlic, the egg and the soaked bread. Season to taste with pepper and salt and a pinch of curry powder. Make small hamburgers of equal size of the mixture and fry them in a pan. Make chips of the parsnips and deep-fry them at 180°C. Dab them dry with paper towels. They form the 'bread' for the hamburgers.

Braise the chopped onion without allowing them to colour. Cut the tomatoes and the red paprikas in big pieces and add them to the onion. After a few minutes of braising add the apple vinegar, the mustard, the sugar, the ketchup, and pepper and salt, and reduce it all to a thick mass. Allow the mixture to cool and then push it through a conical strainer. Season to taste with the whisky-rosemary aroma.

Next make the garlic dressing: push the clove of garlic through a garlic press and mix the mayonnaise with the yoghurt. Season to taste with pepper and salt.

Cut small balls from the courgette and braise them al dente, together with the paprikas which have been cut into pieces.

Put a few parsnip chips on the plate and place a hamburger on top of them. Decorate the hamburger with the braised paprika rings and cover everything with a second layer of parsnip chips. Decorate with the paprika ketchup, courgette balls and the garlic dressing, and spray with whisky-bay leaf aroma.

Whisky-rosemary aroma: Add it to the ketchup.
Whisky-bay leaf aroma : (see p. 166 for the preparation): Spray it strongly on the plate and fleetingly over the whole.

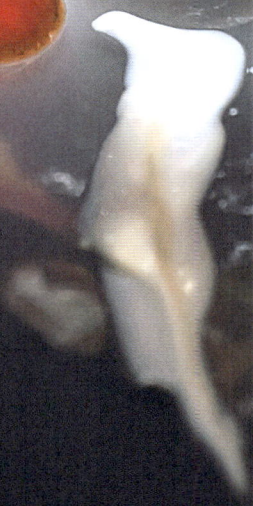

Cod with a puree of haricot beans and new potatoes

Ingredients:

Puree
400 g haricot beans
1 small green pepper
1 finely chopped onion
1 crushed clove of garlic
1 litre herb broth
1 twig of rosemary
2 tablespoons oregano
grated zest of 1/2 lemon
whisky-rosemary aroma
100 g butter
pepper and salt

200 g small new potatoes
pepper and salt
thyme
600 g cod fillet with skin
1 broccoli

Preparation:

Soak the haricot beans overnight in water. Rinse them well and leave them to drain in a colander.

Remove the seeds from the chilli pepper and cut the pepper fine. Sauté it together with the onion and the garlic. Next add the beans and the herb broth. Add the herbs and the grated zest of the lemon and bring it all to the boil. Take care to keep the beans whole. Pour the beans through a strainer and keep the cooking liquid. Puree the beans roughly and add a splash of whisky-rosemary aroma. Stir the butter through it, so that it becomes a smooth puree. Season with pepper and salt.

Boil the new potatoes till done. Halve them and fry them crisp in the pan. Season them with pepper, salt and thyme.

Divide the cod fillet into equal pieces and fry these with the skin side down. Put them in the oven for 7 minutes till done. Put the broccoli florets in the blender and mix them till fine. Blanch them for a few seconds in salted water. Draw a stripe of white bean puree on the plate and put the cod fillet on it. Cover the fillet with the broccoli and finish off with the new potatoes. Decorate with a few remaining beans and a sprig of fresh rosemary.

Tip: to get a smoked effect you can put some sticks of smoked bacon in the puree.

Whisky-rosemary aroma: Mix it into the puree.

Coriander

We know coriander in the shape of dried seeds or fresh leaves. Both are widely used, particularly in the oriental cuisine. It grows in warmer eastern and southern countries, but with a little bit of shelter you can also sow and grow it in Europe. Do this preferably in a sunny position, but you can equally well grow it in pots indoors. It is a superb herb for exotic dishes and is available from most health shops and large stores.

Applications:

You can cut up the fresh leaves in many sauces and salads, in meat and game dishes and in many oriental dishes. Even fish does not shun the coriander leaf.

The seed, often mixed with other herbs and spices, for instance curry powder, is indispensable in oriental cuisine. In the same way, many traditional dishes are finished off with coriander. Coriander is also often included in sachets of dried herbs and spices or combined spice mixes.

Hibiki

Age: 12 years

Region: Japan

Type: fruity. The aroma is fairly balanced. The grainy accent supports the deeper aromas. Exotic fruity tastes mingle with sweet herbs. Evolves towards more spicy touches, but stays sweet. Fairly approachable whisky, can easily be used as an aperitif. Softly sweet herbs and spices are in harmony with the coriander.

Whisky-coriander aroma:

Put the leaves of the coriander plant to infuse in Hibiki whisky. Fill the glass jars generously with freshly cut leaves. Remove the thickest stalks. Allow the leaves to infuse for at least five weeks. The same goes for the seeds, but you need to have a little more patience for the extraction. You can leave this to infuse for two months. You can sprinkle the aroma, spray it or add it. Everything is possible, you can even flambé it.

Sushi with crab

Ingredients:

450 g sushi rice
4 tablespoons rice vinegar
2 tablespoons white sugar
2 teaspoons salt
400 g crab meat
6 sheets of nori (laver)
wasabi
soya sauce
whisky-coriander aroma
fresh coriander leaves

Preparation:

Rinse the rice well in cold water and drain it. Bring the rice to the boil in a pan with water. Turn the heat down and leave the rice on it for 10 to 15 minutes without a lid, till done. Take the pan from the heat, cover the pan and leave the rice to stand for another 10 minutes. Make a mixture of the vinegar, the sugar and the salt and stir it through the rice. After this allow the rice to cool down to room temperature.

Cut 250 g of crab into strips of half a centimetre width. Put a sheet of nori on a bamboo mat and divide a small quantity of rice over it. Leave an edge of 2 cm clear on the sides and at the top. Draw a horizontal stripe of wasabi in the middle. Put the pieces of crab meat just under the stripe. With the aid of the bamboo mat, roll the nori up firmly, starting from the bottom end, and push the ends firmly together. Place the rolls in the refrigerator.

Fifteen minutes before serving, cut the rolls into 2.5 cm portions.

Serve the sushi with a small bowl of soya sauce in which you have dissolved a little wasabi. Use a pipette to sprinkle the whisky-coriander aroma into the sushi or spray the sushi with it.

Arrange the sushi on a plate and decorate it with a few pieces of crab, a fresh coriander leaf, a few drops of soya sauce and wasabi.

Whisky-coriander aroma: Spray of sprinkle the sushi.

Cockles and tuna with artichoke mousse and coriander yoghurt

Ingredients:

4 artichokes
2 dl milk
1 dl vinegar
1 dl cream
150 g butter
2 tablespoons lemon juice
1 kg cockles
1 onion, finely cut
1 celery
1 bunch parsley
1/2 lemon
whisky-coriander aroma
200 g tuna
radishes
1 bunch coriander
2.5 dl yoghurt
pepper and salt
wasabi
4 coriander twigs
ground Emmentaler

Preparation:

Cook the artichokes in water with the milk, vinegar and a pinch of salt. Drain them, take the hearts out of the artichokes and mix them with cream, the melted butter and the lemon juice.

Rinse the cockles in salted water until they are free of sand. Sauté the onion, the celery, the parsley and the lemon, which has been cut in pieces, in a pan. Add the cockles and deglaze with 5 cl whisky-coriander aroma. Leave them to simmer for about 3 minutes till done.

Cut the tuna into cubes and fry them briefly on a high heat. Slice the radishes thinly and spray them with the whisky-coriander aroma.

Season the yoghurt with pepper and salt and mix in the wasabi to your own taste. Cut the leaves of 4 coriander twigs finely and add them to the yoghurt. Scatter strips of milled cheese on a baking tray and bake them golden brown in an oven at 180°C.

Arrange first the artichokes and the baked cheese on the plate. Distribute the tuna and the cockles on top. Finish off with the radishes, a twig of coriander and the yoghurt dressing.

Whisky-coriander aroma: Use it for cooking the cockles and for spraying the radishes.

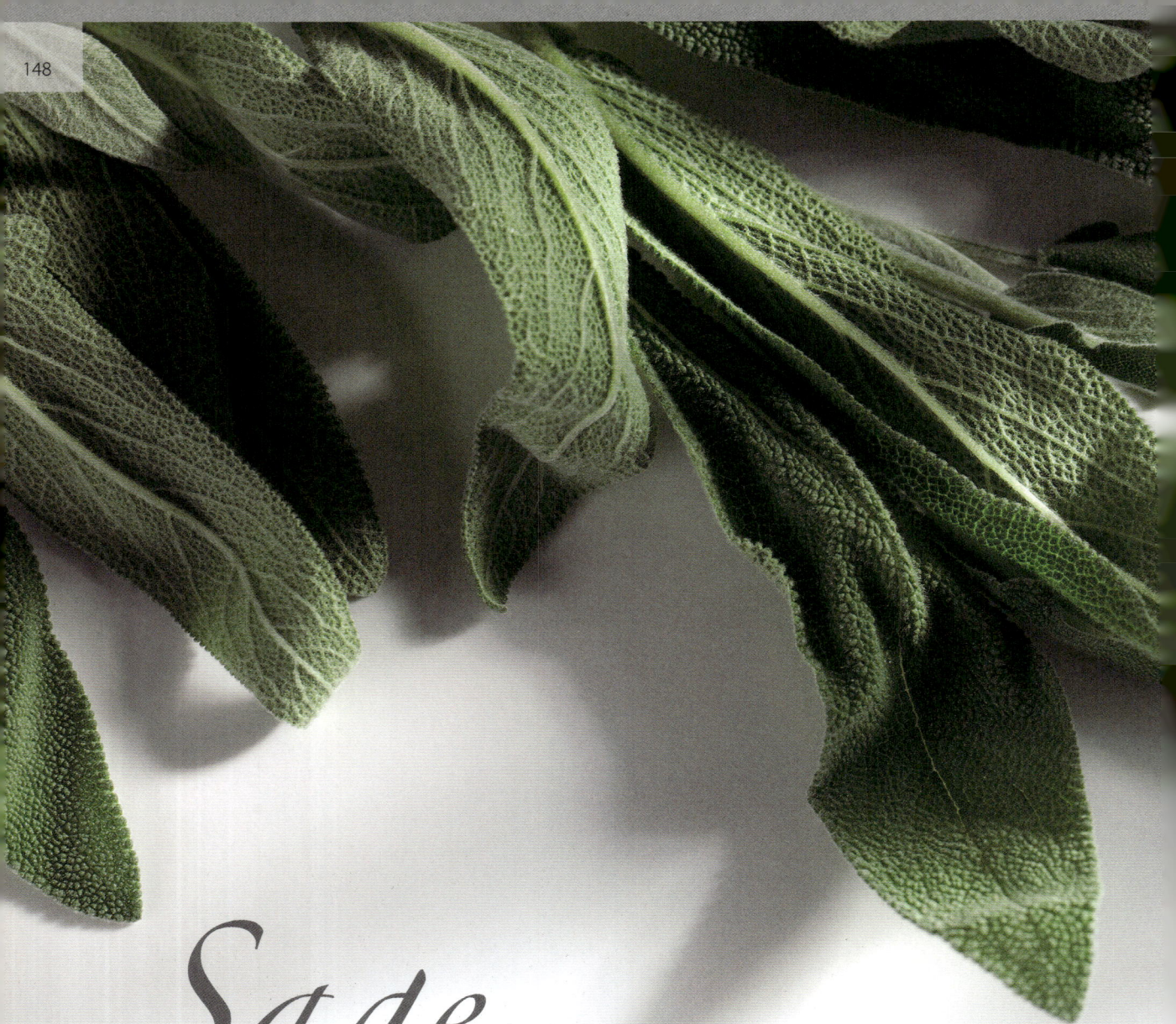

Sage

Like many of the herbs discussed so far, sage is also easy to grow here, but it is mainly cultivated in the Mediterranean area. There are several varieties. Sage is used for perfumes as well as for food. It gives a very specific taste to dishes. It is not quite so popular in the amateur's kitchen, but those who know sage well, will always have it in their cupboard. It is mostly sold and used in dried form.

Sage is recommended as one of the most medicinal herbs, but should not be used in excess.

Applications:

Sage goes with fish, meat and poultry. You can mix it with other herbs and spices or simply use it as a finishing touch. Apparently it is good for the digestion. Cut up the fresh leaves ready for use with roasts or sauces. Also pleasant in cocktails and preserved vegetables.

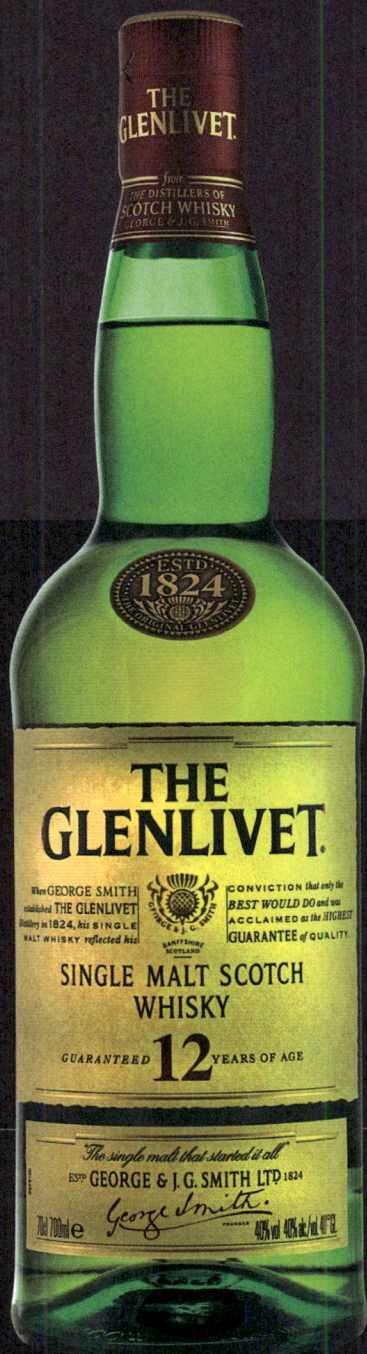

Glenlivet single malt

Age: 12 years

Region: Scotland – Highlands Speyside

Type: An approachable malt. Fruity and sweet with hints towards honey, sweets and grain. Tastes dryer than it smells, which is not experienced as a negative quality. Soft, pleasant aftertaste without surprises. Simplicity is a virtue.
A whisky to win over newcomers. From aperitif to an everyday drink. The balance in this whisky supports and strengthens the sage aroma.

Whisky-sage aroma:

Fill glass jars or bottles with freshly picked sage leaves and fill up with Glenlivet single malt. You will have to smell and taste it regularly. Because of the diversity of sage plants the result is very variable. Some extracts are perfect after two weeks, others may need a month. You can use it with a pipette or vaporizer, or brush on the aroma.

Saltimbocca 'with a difference'

Ingredients:

8 thin veal steaks
whisky-sage aroma
150 g Bolzano salami
pepper and salt
flour
olive oil
butter
1 dl dry white wine
8 spring onions
tagliatelle
garlic powder
300 g ceps
pesto of basil
twigs of fresh sage

Preparation:

Beat the meat flat with a meat hammer. Vaporize it on the top side with whisky-sage aroma. Distribute the salami over the veal steaks and roll them up. Push a wooden stick through them lengthwise to hold the saltimbocca together.

Mix a little pepper and salt into the flour and roll the meat through it. Heat 1 tablespoon olive oil with a knob of butter and fry the meat golden brown. Take the saltimbocca out of the pan, remove the fat from them, and deglaze it with the wine and 5 cl whisky-sage aroma. Put the meat back in the pan and leave it to simmer for a few more minutes.

Melt another small knob of butter among the meat. Cut the spring onions into a slanted julienne and blanch them in salted water.

Cook the tagliatelle in salted water and drain. Pour cold water through the tagliatelle. Reheat in salted butter and season with pepper and garlic powder.

Fry the ceps crisp in olive oil on a high heat.

Arrange the tagliatelle in a turret shape on the plate. Place the saltimbocca on the pesto by it and decorate with the spring onions, a sprig of fresh sage and the ceps.

Tip: Finish the dish off with Parmesan cheeses.

Whisky-sage aroma: Spray it over the meat and use it in the sauce.

Pigeon with rhubarb and pommes dauphines

Ingredients:

Pommes dauphines
5 cl water
5 cl whisky-sage aroma
50 g butter
50 g flour
2 eggs
300 g sweet potato puree
pepper and salt

8 pigeon fillets
2 sticks rhubarb
sugar
sweet white wine

Sauce
2 dl game stock
1 tablespoon Liège pear syrup
5 cl Glendronach single malt
12 years old

a few leaves of sage

Preparation:

First make the pommes dauphines. Bring the water and the whisky-sage aroma to the boil with the butter. Add the flour in one go, and stir it all with a wooden spoon until smooth. Take the pan off the heat and stir in the eggs one by one. Reheat the puree and stir the batter into it. Season to task with pepper and salt. Make quenelles of the batter and deep-fry them till crisp at 180°C.

Fry the pigeon fillets in the pan and season them with pepper and salt. Leave in an oven at 100°C for a few more minutes.

Cut the sticks of rhubarb into equal parts. Put them in an oven dish, scatter sugar over them and pour on the sweet, white wine until they are covered. Place the dish in the oven at 90°C for about two hours.

Next make the sauce. Reduce the game stock with the pear syrup and bring to taste with the Glendronach.

Arrange the potato quenelles and the rhubarb on the plate. Place the pigeon fillets on it and finish off with a sage leaf and the sauce.

Whisky-sage aroma: Use it in the quenelles.

Thyme

There are, again, dozens of different sorts of thyme. They are easy to grow in a moderate or warm climate, also indoors in pots, or outdoors. Thyme can be used very well together with other herbs too. The characteristic smell and taste of thyme is praised all over the world in practically every cuisine. Fresh or dried, as complete twigs or ground, everything is possible. As well as the ordinary thyme which we will discuss here, lemon thyme is also one of the most popular herbs.

Applications:

Thyme is usually incorporated in bouquets garnis for soups, sauces and stews. Fresh twigs can be used in all kinds of meat preparations, as a finishing touch for dishes based on aroma, for fish and in marinades. In short, thyme is used in the kitchen in many ways.

In herbal medicine it is one of the most important herbs against all kinds of illnesses or complaints.

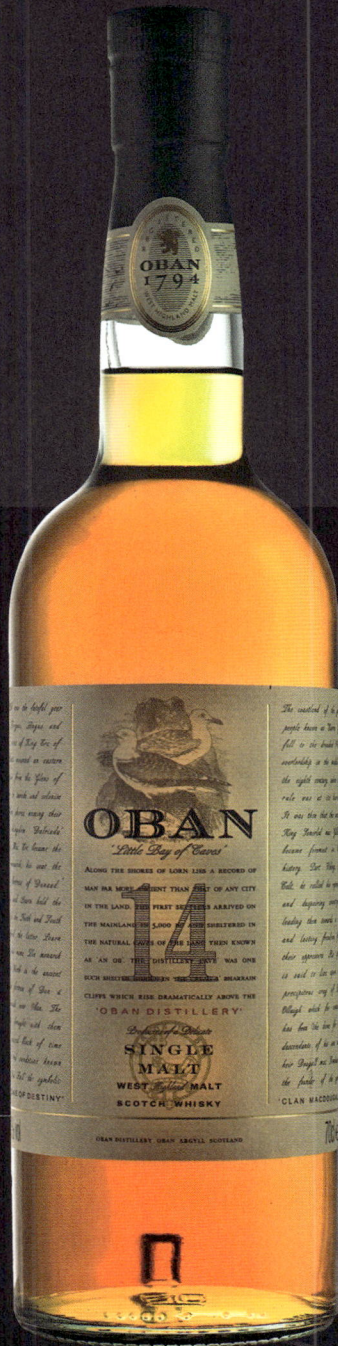

Oban single malt

Age: 14 years

Region: Scotland – Highlands West Coast

Type: Light peat whisky. Caramel with light touches of nuts and grain. The sweet hints lean towards caramel with a floral undertone. Slight hints of toffee towards the end. Nice fin sh with clear coastal and marine accents. Fresh sea breeze.
Reasonably approachable whisky despite its strength. The malt tastes and the thyme blend in a pleasant harmony.

Whisky-thyme aroma:

Simply put the thyme twigs in glass jars or bottles, fill them up with Oban Single malt and give them sufficient time to extract. It can reach the right taste quite quickly, depending on the strength and freshness of the plants used. A month is indicated for infusion. You can remove the twigs when you have reached the required result. Use a vaporizer or pipette at the end of a preparation. You can use the aroma for marinades or as an extra aroma alongside the normal dish. It can be used during cooking or by injecting it.

Black grouse with savoy and chanterelles

Ingredients:

2 grouse (drawn and plucked
by the poulterer)
pepper and salt
100 g blueberries
1 dl whisky-thyme aroma
3 tablespoons sugar
3 tablespoons cherry beer
15 ml red wine vinegar
100 ml poultry stock
2 juniper berries
butter
1/4 savoy cabbage
farm butter
250 g chanterelles

Preparation:

Heat the oven to 200°C. Season the grouse both inside and outside with pepper and salt. Brown them in a pan and then put them in the oven for about 10 minutes. Take them out of the oven and leave them to rest in a warm place for another 5 minutes.

Marinate the blueberries for an hour in the whisky-thyme aroma with the sugar. Next put them in a pan, pour the cherry beer over them and cook them till done. Clear the fat off the pan with the grouse and add the wine vinegar, the poultry stock, the crushed juniper berries and 3/4 of the marinated blueberries. Leave to reduce for a few minutes and mix it all. Push the sauce through a conical strainer and stir in a knob of butter. Season to taste with pepper and salt. Add the remainder of the blueberries to the sauce. Blanch the savoy cabbage in salted water, drain it and sauté it in farm butter. Clean the chanterelles and fry them briefly on a high heat.

Arrange the grouse on the plate and finish off with the savoy, the blueberry sauce, the chanterelles and some whole berries.

Tip: Finish off with a puree of Jerusalem artichoke.

Whisky-thyme aroma: Use it in the marinade of blueberries.

Goat's cheese with chicory, French beans and apple

Ingredients:

8 fresh little goat's cheeses
whisky-thyme aroma
16 slices bacon
2 chicons of chicory
1 Jonagold apple
lemon juice
200 g French beans

Vinaigrette
2/4 grapeseed oil
1/4 walnut oil
1/4 apple vinegar
pepper and salt

1 tablespoon pine nuts
various edible flowers
fresh twigs of thyme

Preparation:

Heat the oven to 180°C. Rub whisky-thyme aroma into the cheeses and wrap each one in a slice of bacon. Cut the chicory and the apple in julienne and sprinkle them with lemon juice to stop them discolouring. Blanch the beans briefly in salted water.
Next make the vinaigrette. Mix the oils and the vinegar and season to taste with the pepper and salt.
Make a salad with the vegetables and the fruit and finish off with the pine nuts and the flowers.
Bake the goat's cheeses in the oven and place them on the salad. Decorate with a fresh sprig of thyme.

Whisky-thyme aroma: Rub it on the cheeses.

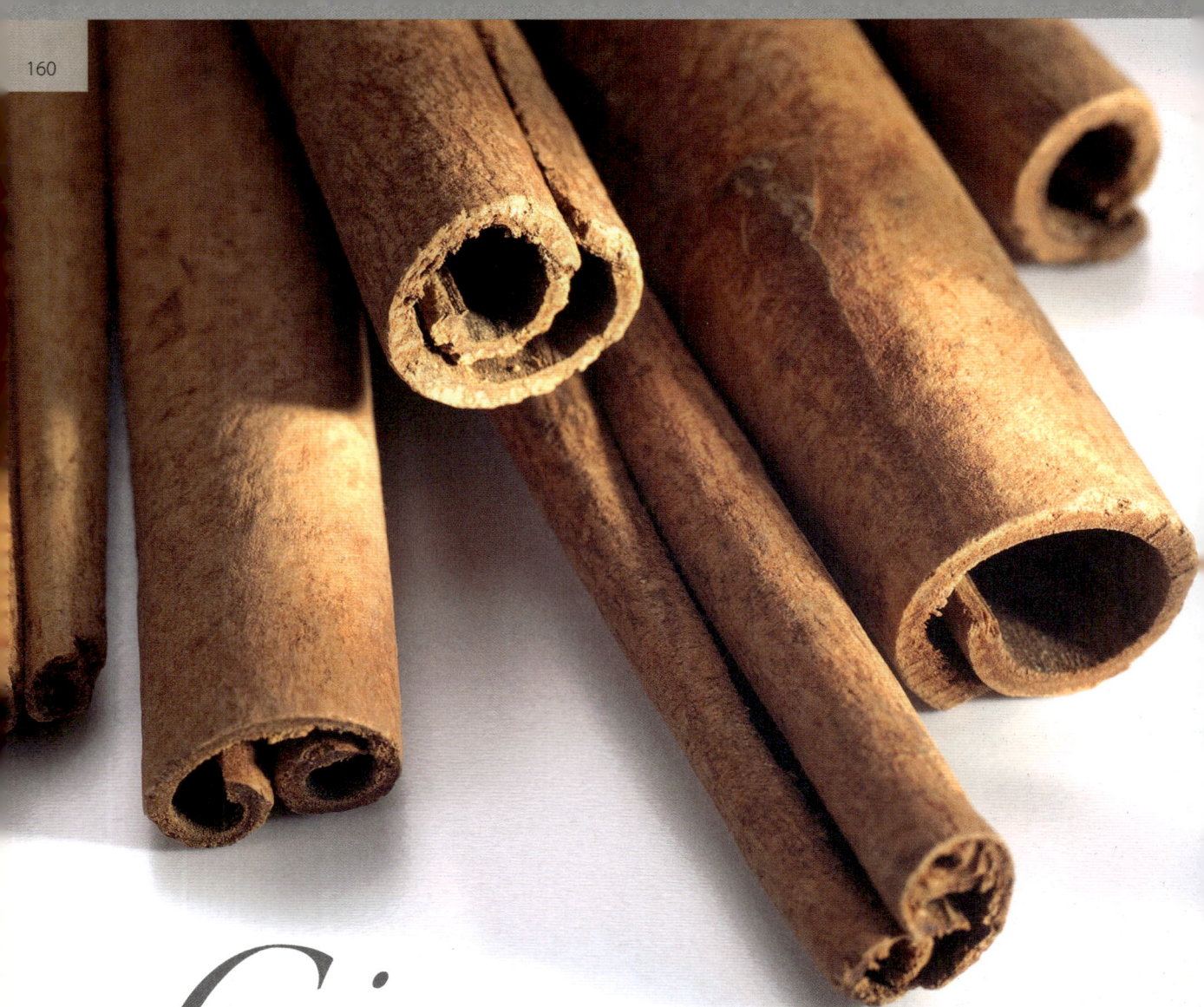

Cinnamon

Cinnamon is made of the dried bark of the cinnamon tree. Obviously from different Asiatic countries different crops of cinnamon are imported. The most prevalent sorts have a very pronounced taste palette. Cinnamon sticks can in many cases be replaced by ground cinnamon. Cinnamon is one of the most recognizable taste enhancers and is popular everywhere.

Applications:

Best known to most of us is rice pudding and apple tart with cinnamon, but there are all kinds of desserts and hot fruit dishes that have been seasoned with cinnamon. In the modern cuisine more and more exotic tasting spices are used, including cinnamon. Just think of turnips fried in cinnamon, or black pudding with cinnamon. The possibilities are really unlimited for creative cooks.

Aberlour

Age: 10 years

Region: Scotland – Highlands Speyside

Type: Sherry maturation. Local fruit, apples stewed in brown sugar. Mild wood touches with nuts and caramel. Nice, full, pleasant touches of sherry with hints of raisins. Balanced and rich aftertaste.
Stewed local fruit touches and cinnamon make up the strength of the extract.

Whisky-cinnamon aroma:

Making a cinnamon aroma is best done with some careful planning. Leave the cinnamon sticks to infuse for three weeks on Aberlour single malt. The extract needs to be processed quickly, don't leave it standing for too long. If you leave the cinnamon sticks to infuse for too long in the whisky, you will have a cloudy result, which does not look appetizing. Use the aroma to spray, sprinkle, spread, inject, and flambé desserts. Much is possible with this aroma.

Duck with turnips and kumquats

Ingredients:

4 ducks' breasts (magret de canette)
2 dl water
1 cinnamon stick
15 kumquats
50 g gelling sugar
1 tablespoon orange vinegar
1 dl game stock
2 tablespoons orange juice
6 turnips
ground cinnamon
pepper and salt
whisky-cinnamon aroma

Preparation:

Make a few light slashes in the skin of the duck breasts. Sear the duck breasts on the skin at a high heat. Turn them over and fry them for another 2 minutes. Next put the pan in an oven at 200°C for 7 minutes. Finally rest the meat for a few minutes in a warm place.

Bring the water to the boil with the cinnamon stick. Add the kumquats and leave them to cook for half an hour. Add the jelly sugar and leave everything to boil for another 5 minutes on a high heat.

Remove the fat from the pan and deglaze with the orange vinegar. Add the game stock and the orange juice and leave it to reduce for a moment. Add the kumquat jelly to it.

Hollow four turnips and blanch the outsides al dente. Cut the other two turnips in brunoise and blanch them. Drain them and fry them till crisp on a high heat. Season with ground cinnamon, pepper and salt. Flambé with the whisky-cinnamon aroma.

Fill the turnips with the fried brunoise. Arrange on the plate a few slices of duck breast and add the turnips, the sauce and a little ground cinnamon.

Whisky-cinnamon aroma: Use it to flambé.

Pear with a chocolate crisp and pear foam

Ingredients:

Pear foam
300 g pear pulp
100 g cream
50 g coconut milk

Chocolate crisp
100 g butter
100 g sugar
100 g egg white
60 g flour
40 g cocoa powder

4 wild stewing pears (Giese-man)
50 cl red wine
2 tablespoons vanilla sugar
200 g sugar
3 cloves
lemon juice
1 tablespoon cornflour
whisky-cinnamon aroma
2 sheets filo pastry
4 balls of pear ice
1 egg yolk
ground cinnamon
sticks of cinnamon

Preparation:

First make the pear foam. Push all ingredients through a fine sieve. Put the juice in a syphon and use two cartridges.

Next make the chocolate crisp. Mix everything well. Stretch out the dough to the shape required. Bake for 5 minutes to finish in an oven at 180°C.

Peel the pears, but leave the stalks on. Bring the red wine, the vanilla sugar, the sugar, the cloves and the lemon juice to the boil. Remove the cloves and add the pears. Leave the pears on low heat until they are done. Take 250 ml of the cooking liquid and bring it back to the boil. Make a custard of the cornflour with 2 tablespoons whisky-cinnamon aroma and add it to the cooking liquid. Allow the sauce to bind.

Cut the filo pastry into two equal parts. Add the balls of pear ice, fold the pastry round them to shut in the ice and brush them with egg yolk. Bake them briefly in a hot oven (250°C).

Arrange them on the plate with a little pear sauce, and on top of it the foam of pear and coconut. Put the pear on top of it and decorate with the filo pastry with the ice cream and the chocolate crisp. A little ground cinnamon and cinnamon sticks will complete this to perfection.

Inject the pear with the whisky-cinnamon aroma.

Whisky-cinnamon aroma: Add this to the sauce and inject it into the pear.

Bay

Mother's stews without a bay leaf would have been unthinkable. We all know the dried leaves of the bay tree. Very likely this will be the first herb the young are consciously aware of. Very many amateur cooks use just a little too much bay, so that the subtle touch of this herb is sometimes lost. In the correct dosage bay certainly qualifies as one of the great taste enhancers in the world of herbs. The best way to grow bay is in pots, which you can bring inside if there is a severe frost. The dried leaves need to be vacuum packed or kept in a well closed glass jar.

Applications:

Bay can be used in stews of meat or game, but also in some soups and certainly in various sauces. Bay is also nice in aromatic broths, fish dishes, vegetable dishes and marinades.

Highland Park

Age: 12 years

Region: Scotland – Orkney Mainland

Type: Lightly smoked. Sweet smoked hints of caramel with floral touches. Scent of dried heather supported by a waft of fruity sweets. At the end slight hints of the sea. Powerful rich aftertaste. A whisky full of character but also approachable. The floral touches go very well with bay.

Whisky-bay aroma:

This aroma is the easiest to make. Fill a glass bottle or jar with plenty of bay leaves and the whisky and simply leave it to infuse. You can leave it perfectly well in the pots after extraction. You can sprinkle, spray and spread, and inject it, and use it in marinades.

Rabbit with dried gingerbread and spiced biscuits ('speculaas')

Ingredients:

4 tablespoons raisins
Glenfarclas 12 years old single malt
8 small onion rings
1 shallot
1 dl rabbit stock
gingerbread
4 rabbit fillets
whisky-bay aroma
spice mixture (pepper, salt, nutmeg, cinnamon, saffron)
2 tablespoons ground speculaas

Preparation:

Soak the raisins in the whisky.
Braise the onions. Chop the shallot finely and braise it. Deglaze with the rabbit stock. Reduce this for a few minutes and add the raisins.
Cut the gingerbread in paper-thin slices and dry these for about 3 hours in an oven at 60°C.
Remove the membranes from the rabbit fillets, coat the fillets with the herb mixture, and fry them briefly. Put them for a few minutes in an oven at 180°C until they are done.
Sprinkle the fillets with whisky-bay aroma. Arrange a few pieces of rabbit on the plate with the gingerbread and the raisins. Finish off the plate with ground spiced biscuits and the onion rings.

Whisky-bay aroma: Sprinkle the fillets with it.

Pig's cheek with red cabbage and pig's trotters croquettes

Ingredients:

Red cabbage
1 dl vinegar
100 g sugar
100 g red cabbage

Pig's trotters croquettes
4 pig's cheeks
4 pig's trotters
200 g braised bacon
salt
thyme
1 bay leaf
1 teaspoon crushed mixed peppercorns
mustard seeds
60 g butter
60 g flour
1 dl veal gravy
3 tablespoons Glenturret single malt whisky
pepper and salt

flour
egg white
panko or breadcrumbs
honey

Preparation:

First prepare the red cabbage. Heat the vinegar and melt the sugar in it. Cut the red cabbage into a fine julienne, pour over the sugared vinegar and put it covered in the refrigerator for 24 hours.

Next make the pig's trotters croquettes. Brown the pig's cheeks in the pan. Simmer the pig's trotters, the pig's cheeks and the bacon for 2 hours in salted water, together with the bay leaf, thyme, crushed peppercorns and mustard seeds. Remove the bacon and the pig's trotters from the stock and chop them up finely. Keep the pig's cheeks separate.

Remove the fat from the stock. Make a roux with the butter and the flour. Take 3 dl of the stock and heat this together with the veal gravy and the whisky. Pour over the roux and stir this to a smooth mass. Mix the meat of the trotters and the bacon through it and season to taste with pepper and salt.

Leave the ragout to set for 24 hours in a cold place. Next make small balls of the ragout, roll them though the flour, eggwhite and panko or breadcrumbs. Deep fry the balls at 180°C.

Lacquer the pig's cheeks with honey and brown them again in the pan. Before serving place the pig's cheeks on the red cabbage. Put the pig's trotter croquet next to it and inject this with whisky-bay leaf aroma.

Whisky-bay aroma: Sprinkle it with a pipette into the croquettes or inject it.

Paprika

Paprikas come in several colours. It is a clearly southern fruit which is often confused with chilli peppers and pigments. They are obviously all fruits from the same family and are often used in the same recipe. All exotic cuisines use paprikas and other peppers. From mild to very spicy varieties they ensure diversity in our modern cuisine. Paprikas are available fresh or in dried form, and even ground to a powder.

Applications:

From southern dishes, winter stews and meat dishes to salads. In short, paprika can give just that extra bit of bite and taste to very many dishes and other preparations. Some people find that fresh paprika does not suit their digestion very well, in which case paprika powder or the extract is a good solution.

Clynelish

Age: 14 years

Region: Scotland – Northern Highlands

Type: Coastal. Caramel; with touches of light smoke and nuts.
Liquorice with hints towards chocolate.
Very rich and powerful aftertaste.
A nice, honest whisky which fits perfectly into the 'after dinner'
picture. Also a pleasant companion of shellfish dishes.
The spicy touches of paprika fit in beautifully with this slightly
stronger whisky.

Whisky-paprika aroma:

Leave the paprikas to infuse for four to five
weeks on Clynelish single malt.
The composition can vary between
ordinary paprika and a few chilli peppers,
according to whether the result should be
more or less spicy. This aroma is certainly
very useful for people who find the fresh
fruit hard to digest. You can vaporize it,
sprinkle or simply just add it, for instance
to a spicy spaghetti.

Frog's legs with Bloody Mary

Ingredients:

16 frog's legs
whisky-paprika aroma
3 egg whites
panko (Japanese breadcrumbs)

Bloody Mary
300 g vine tomatoes
25 cl tomato juice
3 tablespoons vodka
whisky-paprika aroma
juice of 1 lime
1 tablespoon ketchup
1/2 teaspoon Worcester sauce
1/2 teaspoon sugar
tabasco
ground pepper
coriander
celery salt
celery sticks
paprika

Preparation:

Halve the frog's legs, rub in some whisky-paprika aroma and coat them with egg white and panko. Deep-fry the frog's legs.
Next make the Bloody Mary. Mix everything and season to taste with tabasco, pepper, coriander and celery salt. Vaporize the glass with whisky-paprika aroma.
Pour the cocktail into the glass and finish off with a small celery stick. Arrange this on a plate and finish off with a little green and finely chopped paprika as decoration.

Whisky-paprika-aroma: Vaporize the glass, and rub the frog's legs with it.

Sucking calf with spring roll and sweet and sour sauce

Ingredients:

4 sucking calf crown roast portions
pepper and salt
honey
whisky-paprika aroma

Sweet and sour sauce
1 tablespoon oil
2 tablespoons sugar
3 tablespoons vinegar
1 teaspoon corn flour
1 tablespoon whisky-paprika
aroma
2 tablespoons tomato puree

Spring roll
2 spring onions
100 g carrots
0.5 clove garlic
100 g soya been sprouts
100 g peas
2 tablespoons sweet chilli sauce
soya sauce
1 tablespoon Indonesian soya
sauce
8 sheets filo pastry

paprika powder
soya bean sprouts
spring onions

Preparation:

Sear the sucking calf crowns in the pan. Season to taste with pepper and salt and rub in honey. Inject them with whisky-paprika aroma. Transfer to the oven at 180°C till done.
Make the sweet and sour sauce. Heat the oil and melt the sugar in it. Deglaze with vinegar. Stir the cornflour and whisky-paprika aroma into a little pap and use this to thicken the sauce. Finish off with the tomato puree.
Next make the spring roll. Cut the spring onions and carrots in julienne. Crush the garlic clove. Stir-fry the vegetables in a pan and spoon the chilli sauce, the soya sauce and the Indonesian soya sauce through it. Sweat out the liquid. Make spring rolls with the filo pastry and the filling.
Use water to glue the edges together and deep-fry the spring rolls for a few minutes in oil.
Halve the spring rolls and arrange them on a plate. Place the sucking calf crown near it and finish off with a few drops of sauce, paprika powder, soya been sprouts and spring onions.

Whisky-paprika-aroma: Use the aroma in the sauce and inject it into the meat.

Citrus fruits

There are very many citrus fruits and in fact they are all suitable for creating aromas based on malt whisky. The variation in tastes of citrus fruits even makes it possible to make several aromas. For instance, clementines or mandarins will offer a completely different taste pattern than an ordinary orange. Tangelo, better known by its varieties Minneola and Orlando, has again a much more pronounced taste.

Applications:

Citrus aromas can add an extra dimension to an ocean of preparations. The familiar taste and scent lend themselves to perfect taste harmonies. For starters and main courses as well as desserts, citrus fruits are attractive taste enhancers. For various cocktails and soft drinks, sauces, meat and poultry an orange aroma is more suitable. You can also use it for exotic as well as everyday dishes. Citrus fruits turn up everywhere: in marinades, sprayed on, or simply added. The use of citrus extracts or citrus liqueurs (for instance Grand Marnier, based on orange aroma) to flambé dishes is indisputable.

Strathisla

Age: 12 years

Region: Scotland – Highlands Speyside

Type: Sweetish, fruity. Caramel with light touches of citrus.
Clear fruity taste with hints towards malt. Slight hints of butter-
scotch and softwood.
Nice round finish. Approachable whisky for a wide public.
Tasty harmony between the fruit touches in the whisky and the
citrus fruits.

Whisky-orange aroma:

Cut the orange peel into strips of
1/2 cm. Put them in a glass jar or bottle.
Fill up with Strathisla single malt. To a
100 cl jar add 1 sachet vanilla sugar.
Leave it to infuse for four weeks or
longer. Remove the peel when the
required result has been achieved.
It can be kept for a long time.

Foie gras with chicory and a honey jelly

Ingredients:

1 dl sweet wine
3 tablespoons honey
2 leaves of gelatine
4 small chicons of chicory
1 tablespoon sugar candy
2 tablespoons whisky orange aroma
2 tablespoons Portwood matured single malt
3 tablespoons demi-glace sauce
2 tablespoons orange juice
roll of foie gras (circa 320 g)
ground spiced biscuits (speculaas)
4 chocolate sticks
citrus zest

Preparation:

Heat the sweet wine with the honey. Mix the pre-soaked gelatine leaves into it. Leave it all to set in the refrigerator.
Cut the chicory in julienne and colour it in a pan with the sugar candy.
Deglaze this with the whisky-orange aroma. Leave the chicory to cool down.
Reduce the whisky, the demi-glace and the orange juice to the thickness of a sauce.
Roll the foie gras roll through the ground spiced biscuit. Divide it into small cylinders of foie gras and make a little hole in the middle. Place a chocolate stick in it without breaking it. Finish off with the chicory, the sauce and a little zest.

Tip: Orange preserve and raisins complete the dish.

Whisky-orange aroma: Deglaze the chicory with it.

Melon balls with orange flan

Ingredients:

1/4 litre milk
1/4 litre orange juice
1 vanilla pod
4 eggs
100 g sugar
1 melon
whisky-orange aroma
1 banana
1 dl orange juice
1 tablespoon sugar

Caramel
150 g granulated sugar
25 g water
25 g whisky-orange aroma
a little citrus zest

Preparation:

Bring the milk, the orange juice and the vanilla pod to the boil. Beat the eggs with the sugar till white and pour in the hot milk. Return this to the heat and carry on stirring with a spatula until the flan binds. Pour this into small moulds and let it cool down.

Make small balls of half the melon and marinate these in the whisky-orange aroma. Mix the other half of the melon with the banana, the orange juice and the sugar to a soft sauce and put it through a sieve.

Next make the caramel. Bring the ingredients to the boil and carry on boiling until a caramel forms. Pour the caramel over the flan.

Arrange on the plate a few pieces of flan, a few melon balls and the zest. Finish off with the caramel and fruit sauce.

Tip: Use macaroons and coconut to give the dish a crisp touch.

Whisky-orange aroma: Marinate the melon with it.

Juniper berry

The hardy plant of the juniper berry can grow almost any-where. The juniper berry is well-known as a taste enhancer in our production of gin. There are several varieties, from small, low plants to real trees. The ripe fruits are harvested and dried, vacuum-packed or kept in well-closed jars.

will tolerate the taste input of the juniper berry. Finishing desserts with a soft touch of this flavour can be magical. It is also a tasty addition to many marinades.

Applications:
In addition to its use in all kinds of drinks and cocktails, the juniper berry can add a great deal of taste to game dishes and pies. Vegetables too, particularly many cabbage dishes,

Dalmore

Age: 15 years

Region: Scotland – Northern Highlands

Type: Fruity sherry cask maturation. Mild, sweet touches of wood mingle in the nose with raisins and caramel. Rich taste of sweets, sherry, berries and a hint of citrus. Towards the end there are a few more hints of chocolate and nuts. Strong, pleasantly rich finish. Approachable and balanced. Suited to every whisky bar. The hints of forest fruits and berries in the whisky mingle with the juniper berry tastes.

Whisky-juniper berry aroma:

Nothing is easier that this aroma. Fill a glass jar or bottle with dried juniper berries. Fill up with Dalmore single malt and after two weeks you will already have a result, but the aroma can easily be left to infuse for up to five weeks. If necessary the aroma can afterwards be filtered through a coffee filter. You can use this whenever you like, because it can be kept for quite a long time (for several months).

Venison with cranberries and beetroot chips

Ingredients:

4 venison steaks
whisky-juniper berry aroma
pepper and salt
1 raw beetroot
coarse sea salt
1 cooked beetroot

Sauce
50 g cranberries
sugar
1 dl game stock
whisky-juniper berry aroma
100 g sugar
100 g sea salt
2.5 cl Caol Ila whisky

Preparation:

Inject the venison steaks with whisky-juniper berry aroma and fry them rare in the pan. Season them with pepper and salt.

Peel the beetroot, cut it in paper-thin slices and leave them to dry out for 20 minutes between two sheets of kitchen paper. Deep-fry them till crisp at 180°C and put some coarse sea salt on them. Cut the cooked beetroot into a coarse brunoise and marinate this in whisky-juniper aroma.

Next make the sauce. Coat the cranberries with sugar and cook them till done in the game stock. Season them extra to taste with whisky-juniper berry aroma.

Mix the sugar and the salt and sprinkle with the whisky. Leave this to dry for a few hours in an oven at 60°C. Scatter a little over the fried venison.

Arrange the venison steaks with the beetroot and the beetroot chips on the plate. Finish off with a line of sauce.

Tip: Finish off with spring onions and a mousse of parsnips and celeriac.

Whisky-juniper aroma: Inject the venison steak and finish off the sauce with it.

Sucking pig with sauerkraut and small marrowbones

Ingredients:

4 small marrowbones
2 sucking pig fillets
milk
Szechuan pepper
300 g sauerkraut

4 thin slices of smoked bacon
whisky-juniper berry aroma
1 tablespoon sugar
10 ml walnut oil
100 g pearl onions
cayenne pepper
3 tablespoons Dalmore whisky
1 dl veal gravy
a few juniper berries

Preparation:

Wrap the marrowbones in aluminium foil. Poach them for 10 minutes in salted water. Desalt the fillets for 30 minutes in milk. Next dab them dry, season them with Szechuan pepper and put them in an oven at 160°C until done. Spoon the sauerkraut into round moulds which are clad with bacon. Heat them for 7 minutes in an oven at 160°C. Vaporize with whisky-juniper berry aroma.

Heat the sugar and the walnut oil and caramelize the pearl onions in them. Season them with cayenne pepper. Deglaze it all with the whisky and the veal gravy. Reduce everything slowly to 2/3 of the quantity.

Arrange the bacon with the sauerkraut and the marrowbones. Decorate with the pearl onions, a few juniper berries and the gravy.

Whisky-juniper berry aroma: Vaporize the sauerkraut.

> List of the whisky and herb aromas and the recipes accompanying them

www.lannoo.com

Register your name on our website and we will regularly send you a newsletter with information on new books and interesting, exclusive offers.

The Glengarry
Sint-Baafsplein 32
B-9000 Gent
Tel. + 32 9 233 58 98
www.glengarry.be
robert.minnekeer@telenet.be

De Cluysenaer
Kluizendorpstraat 82
B-9940 Ertvelde-Kluizen
Tel. + 32 9 357 73 37
www.cluysenaer.be
info@cluysenaer.be

Author: Bob Minnekeer
Recipes: Stef Roesbeke and Bob Minnekeer
Photography: Andrew Verschetze and Joris Devos
Layout: Joris Devos
Translation: Alastair and Cora Weir

If you have comments or questions, you can contact our editors:
redactielifestyle@lannoo.com.

© Lannoo Publishers, Tielt, 2011
D/2011/45/290 – NUR 440 and 447
ISBN: 978 90 209 9607 4